The Fourth Witch

A Memoir of Politics and Sinning

By

Richard Morgan

Former Speaker of the North Carolina

House of Representatives

ISBN: 978-0-615-26367-0

Library of Congress Control Number: 2008910870

For Cindy with love,
and in memory of Mary Crain Morgan.

PROLOGUE
Politics and Sinning

Most times, when a fellow runs for office and you ask him, *Why*, he'll take a deep breath and give you a high-sounding reason – like he's going to stop the ice caps melting, save family values, or single-handedly end poverty.

But I can tell you – first hand – most politicians have earthier goals: Like greed, vanity or ambition.

A few years ago we elected a farmer to the United States Senate. When hog prices dropped he sponsored a bill to subsidize trade with the Russians – to sell them more hogs.

The biggest Bible thumper I served with in the House – a hard-shell fundamentalist who taught at *The Gospel Light Christian*

School – took a fifty-thousand-dollar bribe to vote with the same Democrats who'd killed every bill he'd introduced to ban abortion.

Another legislator owned a multi-million dollar beer and wine distributorship and saw nothing wrong with serving on the House Committee that regulates alcohol.

Another legislator managed a successful architectural firm that received ten million dollars in unbid state contracts.

Once, when I was Speaker, leaving the House Chamber I came face to face with an old man, a county commissioner wearing khakis, a denim shirt and a thick-soled pair of boots.

I stopped, nodded and asked, 'So, tell me, how did you get into politics?'

He scratched his head then grinned. 'Well, that was simple – like most young people I was interested in sinning.'

'You learn much?'

'Probably not as much as you.'

He smacked his lips. 'You know ole Jim Hunt?'

After Governor Hunt was elected the third time Republicans and Democrats in the House had a knock-down, drag-out fight over the budget and one spring night, dead set on breaking the deadlock, Hunt walked out of the Governor's Mansion, trekked down the block to the condominium I shared with House Speaker Harold Brubaker and strolled through the door carrying a six-pack of hard full-sugar Pepsi under his arm.

A Republican couldn't be too careful when dealing with Governor Hunt. One moment he'd be all charm and the next, as soon as you let your guard down, he'd pounce and before you could stop your lips from moving out of a spirit of comity and good will you'd agree to vote for a bill you hadn't seen yourself supporting in a thousand years.

What stopped Hunt dead in his tracks that night was one of those new vibrating recliner chairs from Sharper Image my wife had given me after I won my first election. Hunt settled all the way back in that chair and it started to hum and he grinned, 'Mighty fine,' and any orneriness he felt flew right out the window.

We put steaks on the grill and passed the next three and a half hours without a harsh word as Hunt drank that whole six-pack of hard Pepsi.

Ten years later, looking back at the old county commissioner, I said carefully, 'Yes sir. I knew Governor Hunt.'

'That boy give you a hard time?'

I remembered the first morning Hunt called and woke me out of a sound sleep just after the crack of dawn to talk about a bill.

'He tended to burn the midnight oil and forget normal folks sleep at night.'

He grunted. 'That boy always did have a red-hot passion for politics.'

'There I'd have to say you're wrong.'

The ridges in the old man's face hardened. 'I reckon you figure you got a better explanation?'

'I'd say the reason for that passion was pure sugar.'

⌘

My first ten years in politics I didn't win an election. Over the next twenty years I didn't lose one. I'd like to think that's because I figured politics out but the truth is like oceans and rivers politics is governed by tides and what happened was the tides turned and started flowing in Republicans' direction and in spite of the mistakes we made carried us with them.

By 1994 those tides were flowing so strong and deep, despite Jim Hunt, we elected a Republican majority to the State House for the first time since 1896.

I don't know who that shocked most: the governor, a legion of Raleigh lobbyists or the sixty-eight Republicans who in defiance of logic and common sense woke up the morning after the election in control of the State House.

We promptly elected Harold Brubaker Speaker and Harold appointed me Chairman of the Rules Committee which doesn't sound like much but it was back then because of Rule 36-A – a rule that said the only way a bill could get to the House floor for a vote was if the Rules Chairman put it on the calendar.

You might think that would have made the Rules Chairman popular but you'd be dead wrong. I spent the next four years telling people 'No' as in 'No, the House is never going to vote on your bill.'

In 1998 when we lost the majority I was elected Republican Leader in the House. Four years later I ran for Speaker and after losing eight straight Roll Call votes – I got just five votes each time – was elected on the ninth ballot.

President Reagan once said that watching politics from the inside is like watching civilization with its pants down. I had a ring-side seat for sixteen years. I saw larger-than-life characters like Jesse Helms, Jim Hunt, Bill Clinton and Ronald Reagan and less colorful wheel-horses like Jim Holshouser, Jim Martin and Mike Easley.

And I served as Co-Speaker for two years with Jim Black – the Democrat who went to prison.

I testified in front of the State Board of Elections twice, a grand jury once and had a front-row seat for a series of House sex scandals, everything from Leo Daughtry making what was then called an 'inappropriate advance' to a House clerk's niece to Representative Ken Miller making a lot more than an 'inappropriate advance' to a sixteen-year-old intern.

Leo apologized. Miller denied it and was censored.

Once a former Republican Legislator sued another former legislator and I ended up right in the middle of a slander lawsuit. The day I was called to testify in a deposition the plaintiff's lawyer, hammering away glared across the table and asked if I thought his client – Art Pope – was a crook.

I looked back at the lawyer, then at Art.

'No, sir. I don't think Art's a crook. But I don't get the feeling about him I get about Bambi or Old Yeller either.'

Art Pope and I were friends the first two years we served together in the legislature – a decade later he spent a million dollars to defeat me and my House allies.

The thread that runs through our lives is sinning, from the third chapter of Genesis down to modern times. I've never walked in the shoes of a policeman, a Wall Street banker or a soldier. I've never studied the motives of violent criminals, the ravages of rampant greed, or witnessed the scars of war first-hand. But I have seen politics and sinning.

CHAPTER ONE

The Black Hole

I was elected to State House the year Jesse Helms beat Harvey Gantt and won his fourth term in the Senate.

By then I'd been supporting Jesse for eighteen years – back to the time I volunteered in his first campaign in college. Politicians talk a lot about being mavericks. About as good a definition as I've found is supporting Jesse Helms in Chapel Hill.

Back in 1972 the first time Jesse ran like a lot of young people I was interested in politics. Interested. Not enthralled. Or fascinated. Just curious.

What I found out is politics is like one of the black holes scientists say hover at the edges of the universe – when you get too close the gravity coming out of that hole grips you and pulls you in and there's no escape.

Two years after I supported Jesse, when I graduated from college, the gravity pulled me into Bill Steven's campaign for United States Senate.

I'd never thought of political campaigns as a temptation but what I found out is they can be as addictive as a narcotic.

Most folks live by routines. They work nine to five. Eat. Sleep. Go out on Friday night. Go to church on Sunday. But in politics there are no routines. There are no nine-to-five jobs. You work all day and into the night. You work on Saturdays and Sundays. You live in a primordial state where strangers come together and bond and form tribes like Comanche or Sioux – you're down there in that black hole together and the fellowship you share is addictive.

Jesse Helms and Jim Hunt were what I'd call natural politicians. They took to politics like ducks to water. Hunt could roll up his sleeves and wade into a crowd of farmers at a tobacco warehouse like a hog in slop. But Bill Stevens couldn't do that. He and those farmers lived in different worlds and Bill didn't have the guile to try to fool them. He had a golden touch as a businessman. He could read balance sheets and profit and loss statements and wore tailored suits with silk handkerchiefs in the pocket but when he stood up to give a stump speech, well, it was like he was reading one of those financial reports.

Brad Hays, who later ran Jim Martin's campaigns for governor, ran Bill's campaign against Robert Morgan out of three dank, windowless rooms in the basement of the Hilton Hotel on Hillsborough Street in Raleigh.

Brad saw pretty quickly that Bill wasn't going anywhere as a candidate unless he got shed of that boardroom stiffness, so one morning he told me to go to the airport and pick up an expert, flying in from Washington, who was going to turn Bill into a politician over the weekend.

Later, that expert – Roger Ailes – would turn out to be a kind of political genius. He elected George H.W. Bush in 1988 by making one of the funniest ads I ever saw, showing Michael Dukakis sitting in the turret of a tank, wearing what looked like a 1920's Notre Dame football helmet. Later, Roger went on to found Fox News and I guess if it had been possible to turn Bill Stevens into a fire-breathing politician like Jesse Helms, Roger could have done it – but in the end it wouldn't have mattered that year.

There are elections where the tides are running so strong and deep and fast in one direction that nothing you can do matters.

After Watergate, Nixon being impeached and our losing the war in Vietnam those tides spelled doom for the Republicans in 1974 – when the smoke cleared we were left with exactly one Republican in the State Senate and nine in the House. Less than after the Civil War.

We also lost half of our Republican Congressmen including my local Congressman Earl Ruth, who shrugged and summed it up like this: 'Well, I came in with Nixon and I went out with Nixon.'

But Earl didn't end up too badly. After he lost President Ford appointed him Governor of American Samoa where, the way Earl told it, he spent two years sitting on a veranda watching the sunset over the Pacific Ocean while being fanned by natives.

Earl's experience with patronage beat mine hands down.

Twenty-two years old and out of work I needed a job and a Republican from my home town, George Little, got me one in Governor Holshouser's Administration. It was the only patronage job I've ever held and I don't want another.

I spent six months shuffling reports and grants in 'The Governor's Law and Order

Program' then escaped to the Department of Human Resources where I worked for Secretary David Flaherty.

Governor Holshouser's Cabinet was made up of a somber, serious-minded group of Republican businessmen in gray suits who were hardly ever accused of having a sense of humor – the exception was Dave Flaherty.

Looking back Dave must have stuck out like a sore thumb. First, he was a Massachusetts Yankee who'd attended Boston College then moved south to settle in the North Carolina mountains; second, he had one virtue that didn't belong in Governor Holshouser's Cabinet – he could have wrestled alligators and found a way to make it fun.

Dave's great passion, besides politics, was golf and he didn't let little things like rules get in his way. The first time I walked down a fairway with him he tramped into the rough, scowled down at his ball lying in a hole in the high grass, then looked up and grinned and said, "Winter Rules" – which, I gathered, was a set of mountain golfing rules he'd made up out of thin air that said he could move the ball back into the fairway anytime he wanted.

The truth is Dave didn't take golf seriously but Tom Ellis the Raleigh lawyer who ran Jesse's campaigns did. Once Mr. Ellis missed a three-foot putt and what happened next was akin to watching a volcano exploding. He leaned down over his putter bending it like a pogo stick then just when it was about to snap in two he hurled it twenty yards. Then it was like nothing ever happened. He strolled over to the putter, picked it up, put it back in his bag and ambled on to the next tee as peacefully as a lamb.

What Dave was dead serious about was running the Department of Human Resources and he had an eerie way of showing up where he was least expected that drove state bureaucrats crazy.

One night he drove down to the Stonewall Jackson Youth Center, rooted the superintendent out of bed and led him into a boys' dormitory with no air conditioning and the windows sealed shut and a thermostat that said 100 degrees.

Arms waving Dave stamped both feet. 'I heard it but I wouldn't have believed it if I hadn't seen it with my own eyes.' His eyes widened. 'I wish you'd explain one thing to me.'

The superintendent shuffled his feet, thrust his hands into his pockets. 'Tell me what it is and I'll try.'

'How on earth do you figure a sixteen-year-old boy can learn anything during the day when he can't sleep at night?'

The day I started working for Dave he handed me a stack of letters and said, 'There are twenty problems. Your job is to solve them. But, first, you've got to see them. To look every one of those people in the eye.' He sent me on a tour of every state Alcoholic Rehabilitation Center, Psychiatric Hospital and what were then called 'Mental Retardation Centers.'

And I'd never seen anything like it.

I'd grown up in a small town – Southern Pines – where my father sold cars and my mother worked in real estate then in insurance until she opened her own consignment shop, *The White Elephant*.

In high school I'd worked at the only local radio station in town and after graduation, when my friends went to the beach, the station owner sent me up to the new Institute of Radio, Television and Motion Pictures at the University of North Carolina. Sitting on the lawn under a shade tree outside Swain Hall I took one look at Chapel Hill and decided college was the place for me.

The only thing I needed was a pot of money I didn't have.

I went home and enrolled in Sandhills Community College and while working full-time took every course that would transfer to UNC. It took me two years to get back to Chapel Hill but in 1972 I borrowed enough in student loans to cover my tuition, got a job in the law school and enrolled.

But nothing I saw at Chapel Hill prepared me for those state 'Mental Retardation Centers.' It was bedlam. I'd never heard of a hydrocephalic. The politically incorrect term folks used to describe those poor people back then was waterheads. In the first center I met a boy whose head was so swollen his neck just couldn't hold it up, so he had to spend all day anchored to his bed unable to lift his head.

I walked into a recreation room and found myself face to face with a teenage boy fumbling with an alphabet board. Now everyone knows what a baby's walker looks like – imagine a baby walker big enough to hold a teenager with a magnetic board fastened to the front. That boy couldn't walk or talk or write but he could move his feet just enough to roll that walker toward me, then, arms waving, shoulders jerking, head twitching, in an act of pure courage he put enough magnetic letters on that tray to spell out the word "Hello."

It was enough to break your heart.

Back then scientists were just discovering 'wonder drugs' to treat mental illnesses and if David Flaherty did one thing right in his life it was using those drugs to get people out of those institutions and into group homes where they could lead not normal lives but lives a lot better than anything they'd ever known. He opened Duncraig Manor the first 'group home' in North Carolina right up the street from my mother's house. Just about everyone said David had a good idea with those group homes but absolutely everyone within a mile of that home also said, 'Not in my backyard.' Most of Southern Pines was up in arms. One afternoon as I walked down the street a neighbor stopped me and chewed me out.

I waited till he was done then nodded and told him to take an afternoon off from work and go get a good look at the inside of a state Mental Retardation Center then to come back and tell me what he thought.

CHAPTER TWO

Treacheries and Blessings

In 1976 the local Republican Party in Moore County asked me to run for the State House. That may sound like an honor but, I reckon, the truth is they figured no one but a twenty-three-year-old boy would be fool enough to try – because there'd *never* been a Republican elected to the House or much of anything else in Moore County, where there were three Democrats for every Republican.

I lost with 47% of the vote which doesn't sound too bad but it turned out to be another lesson about politics: Politics isn't horseshoes. Close doesn't count. There's no difference between losing by three percent and losing by thirty except it's a little less embarrassing on election night.

After that election I also learned a lesson that's held true for thirty years: A lot of good can come from a defeat. I've lost four elections and every one of them was followed by an unexpected blessing. The blessing in 1976 was I'd been forcibly retired from politics so I had to get a job.

Even back then George Little was a kind of local legend in Republican politics in Moore County. George had served in Governor Holshouser's Cabinet but that had only been a short-term diversion. What George was really interested in was selling insurance and he had a gift for it. George was about six feet, four inches tall and built like a linebacker and years later, Carter Wrenn, who ran Senator Helms' political organization The Congressional Club, told me, 'Richard, you've got to watch George. He's jovial. But never forget he's got the heart of a pirate.'

I took the state insurance exams, got a license and George and I hammered out an agreement: I'd work independently out of a cubbyhole in his office selling insurance and as the "General Agent" he'd get a commission on my sales.

Today, I've still got clients I signed up that first year.

A lot of young people make a terrible mistake when they go into the insurance business. They make their first sale and figure they've learned all they need to know and stop. They never take the next step. I was lucky. I figured out I had to learn the insurance business inside-out. The first two years I worked with George it was like earning my way through college again – I enrolled in the Life Underwriting Training Council and learned everything from the subtleties of modern-day estate planning to the first English underwriters providing insurance for English sailing ships in the 1600s. (Those underwriters founded the first insurance company: Lloyds of London).

⌘

In 1978, I signed on to another campaign and learned one more lesson: Winning can be as treacherous as losing. I ran Jerry Whipple's campaign for sheriff and in a minor miracle for the first time in a hundred years Moore County elected a Republican.

The cause of the treachery was love.

Not Romeo and Juliet love but what I once heard a Baptist preacher call other woman love.

About as soon as Jerry got sworn in he fell head over heels in love with the dispatcher in the sheriff's office. Only no one knew it. Not his wife. Or her husband.

Then one morning Jerry and the dispatcher disappeared. They just vanished. We had a jail full of criminals and no sheriff in sight. Worse, since we couldn't find Jerry we couldn't replace him. He hadn't officially resigned and, legally, he was still the duly elected sheriff.

The blessing that followed that bit of sinning was odd.

As a result of blind dumb luck we finally found out Jerry and the dispatcher had run off to New York and the party leaders got in touch with him long enough for Jerry to say even if we were short a sheriff he wasn't coming home – which everybody took as a back-handed resignation.

We picked the Pinehurst police chief, a Democrat, James Wise, who'd attended the FBI Academy to replace Jerry. Jim Wise was the most popular sheriff ever in Moore County and served for sixteen years, until he retired.

⌘

In 1980 I ran for State House, again, but even before I got started I found out George had the same idea – but how he was going about it was odd. George was circulating petitions to get people to vote for him in bars and honky-tonks like Pygie Pugh's place. Pygie was another local legend. During the day he was a local undertaker but at sundown he'd saunter out the funeral home and mosey down to his bar 'The Inside Club.'

It's hard to say what surprised me most: George thinking circulating petitions in bars made any kind of sense at all or that he didn't bother to tell me about it.

At the time I took it as a mild kind of treachery but, in the end, it turned out to be a blessing too. I moved out of George's office in Southern Pines and pretty soon had my own agency up and running in Pinehurst and it's still there today.

One evening about sundown George came to see me and said like a Dutch uncle that he'd never intended to run, that all he'd been doing was looking out for my best interest, that he'd just wanted to see if I was serious and now he knew I was and he was rock-solid behind me and he'd support me. We shook hands on it in front of two witnesses.

I reckon that night he meant it but a week later he got one of the county commissioners to run against me. I lost the primary but, by then, I was getting a feel for the rhythm of politics so the blessing that followed that defeat wasn't completely unexpected.

CHAPTER THREE

Goats and Pachyderms

After I lost Jerry Blackwelder, my roommate from back when I worked for Dave Flaherty, was managing Gene Johnston's campaign for Congress in Greensboro. I volunteered to help by raising money from political action committees and the next thing I knew I ran head-on into Senator Helms' political organization The Congressional Club.

Back in the early 1970's I had the naïve idea Republicans were one big happy family. But I was dead wrong. Republicans were like the Hatfields and the McCoy's. There were two wings in the party: The Holshouser wing and the Helms wing and they feuded for years.

The folks at The Congressional Club had their own way of describing the riff. They'd talk about 'goats' and 'pachyderms.' The 'pachyderms' were Holshouser supporters. Pachyderms believed in the party first. They were practical, non-ideological and they voted the straight Republican ticket and naturally they got dubbed pachyderms because the Republican symbol is the elephant.

'Goats' was a term of endearment. 'Goats' were Helms supporters. They were conservative, ideological, and didn't give one toot about party politics. 'Goats' voted for the man not the party.

When Jesse used to say he didn't care which party straightened out America as long as one of them did it just drove the pachyderms up the wall because they just couldn't see a Democrat straightening out anything.

The pachyderms were pretty delighted when conservative Democrats like Jesse started voting for Republican candidates but when those Jessecrats decided they wanted a say in who got nominated in Republican primaries that didn't sit too well with the pachyderms at all.

The spark that ignited the powder keg was Ronald Reagan challenging Gerald Ford for President in 1976. Naturally the way the pachyderms saw it no loyal Republican would challenge an incumbent Republican president. The way the goats saw it the fact Gerald Ford was sitting in the White House didn't make one bit of difference.

Governor Holshouser supported Ford and Jesse waded in tooth and toenail for Reagan and it was a good old fashioned, eye-gouging, elbow-throwing primary. Jesse's folks didn't ask any quarter and when it came to electing Reagan didn't offer any either. When the smoke cleared to the pachyderms' amazement Jesse and Reagan had walloped Ford in North Carolina. Then they got another shock. At the Republican State Convention when North Carolina's first Republican governor since 1901 tried to get himself elected delegate to go to the National Convention to vote for Gerald Ford the goats walloped him too.

Next The Congressional Club did something no one had ever seen before in North Carolina. They turned Jesse's 1978 reelection race into a national campaign and raised a whopping $7 million.

As soon as they'd gotten Jesse reelected they set out – in 1980 – to elect Reagan President and a political science professor from East Carolina University no one had ever heard of named John East to the United States Senate.

Now, my friend Jerry Blackwelder had worked in Governor Holshouser's campaign and, naturally, had the idea the Helms people were some sort of devils incarnate. So it came as a shock one day when out of a clear blue sky Jerry said he hated to admit it but after working with the folks at The Club he'd decided they weren't devils at all.

Carter Wrenn, who ran The Club, and I had been at Chapel Hill together though as best either of us can tell we never laid eyes on each other (though Carter says he does remember meeting me, later, in the lobby of a hotel in Asheville the year I was working for Bill Stevens).

Almost everyone who goes to Chapel Hill starts out conservative and ends up liberal but Carter spent four years moving in the opposite direction. I think that was, in part, because he simply ignored the university's recommended curriculum and just studied whatever struck him; and, in part, it was because after a year he got shed of dormitories and moved into a garret apartment which allowed him to ignore most of what happened on campus – but which also brought out an unfortunate anti-social streak.

The second time we met was in his office at The Club and it turned out to be the start of a friendship that's lasted thirty years – though I can't say it's always been a bed of roses. Once we got so tangled up on different sides in a political fight and so mad at each other we didn't speak for seven years. But we also buried the hatchet which is even rarer in politics.

Back then watching the folks at The Congressional Club in action was an education in politics you couldn't get anywhere else on earth.

You could have fitted the whole Democratic and Republican Party Headquarters into The Club's offices in Raleigh and had two floors left over. The entire first floor of The Club was one huge room jammed full of computers – not computers like we see these days but old-fashioned IBM-style computers that filled rooms and had to have special raised floors above the cables connecting them and special air-conditioning to keep them from overheating. Back then that was high technology and when it came to applying it to politics The Club was about ten years ahead of whoever was in second place. They spent more money on those computers than most candidates spent in an entire election.

A few years later when I ran for State House the third time the folks at The Club pushed a button and printed out a list of names of every Republican who'd ever voted in a primary in my district. Then pushed another button and handed me a list of donors in Moore County. Then turned on a printer the size of a small trailer and in thirty minutes printed a letter to every one of those donors saying Jesse was a conservative and I was too and any likeminded conservative could help by sending money. Checks rolled in.

At first to anyone on the outside The Club looked like a dictatorship run by Jesse and Tom Ellis. But before long, just sitting in Carter's office watching, I realized it was a pretty peculiar kind of dictatorship. I never saw anything operate the way The Club did. When they made a TV ad it was like watching ten people having a brawl. They'd argue over every word and syllable like cats and dogs with everybody from the New York pollster to the TV director flailing away then, suddenly, there would be an invisible click and in the blink of an eye they'd all be on the same wavelength and Tom Ellis would look at Carter and say, *Okay, don't just sit there. Get the ad on the air.*

A lot of folks found Jesse's politics too rough-edged and unbending to suit them but like him or not you had to admit he had razor-sharp political instincts. Jesse could be tough as nails. Once I asked John East what it was like to serve in the Senate with Jesse. 'Well,' he grinned, 'Jesse's a brawler' – and he meant it as a compliment. Jesse wasn't afraid of a fight. But at the same time if you were just sitting in the room with him and he didn't have politics on his mind Jesse could be as charming as any fellow I ever laid eyes on.

Tom Ellis, on the other hand, never bothered to charm anyone. Mr. Ellis is one of the few people I ever met in politics who had just one pure and simple motive: He was an ideologue. A true believer. A man with a mission and that can be pretty dangerous because once a fellow sets out to save the world something frightening happens to his eyesight. He starts to see everything in black and white. The world divides into his friends and his enemies and he loses any inclination he ever had to see both sides. But Tom Ellis also had, when it came to politics, a zigzag streak of lightning in his brain.

The other genius at The Club – their secret weapon – was the pollster Arthur Finkelstein. Even in a room full of characters Arthur stood out. He'd walk through the door carrying a poll tucked under his arm and take off his shoes and unfasten his tie, leaving the ends dangling, and start pacing up and down in his stocking feet – then Tom Ellis would growl, *Okay, you've told me about the poll. Now tell me the ad*, and without blinking Arthur would go into a kind of trance and just dictate a thirty-second ad.

Arthur Finkelstein and Tom Ellis were like two forces of nature; when you put them in the same room it was like two electrical fields crashing together and crackling and what they gave off like sparks was ideas.

Carter's gift was what he could do with the ideas. He had two characteristics you don't find often in one person. He could write. And he was organized. He could look at a TV script and see how to put a hundred pieces into place – cameras, directors, editors – to get those words off a sheet of paper onto a piece of video and onto the air at a TV station.

Once I asked him how The Club got built and he said, 'Well, Arthur laid out the structure – like the blueprint for a building – and I just built it.' Tom Ellis was the one who decided The Club would go into direct mail fundraising and Carter was the one who figured out how to use it to raise a hundred million dollars.

But money wasn't the secret of The Club's success.

Ideas were The Club's currency and in 1980 the idea they had their teeth into was the Panama Canal. They must have run ten thousand ads to elect John East that all said one thing – Bobby Morgan voted to give away the canal. It got so bad most of us watching those ads started hollering, 'Alright, by God, we got it. Anyone who's not deaf and dumb knows how Morgan voted.'

But just when Tom Ellis started thinking about taking those ads off the air Arthur Finkelstein would come to Raleigh with a poll and point to a number and say, *See, three hundred thousand, or two hundred thousand, or one hundred thousand people still haven't seen that ad. Keep running it.*

Then just before the election Arthur made a mistake.

Mr. Ellis later said the problem was Arthur was a big Yankees fan and got his mind on the World Series and off politics – whatever the reason one night Arthur called Carter and Tom from a pay phone in Yankee

Stadium and gave them the bad news. They needed a new ad.

Mr. Ellis growled, 'About what?' and Arthur said, 'I'm not sure and I've got to go to the ballgame.'

The next morning Tom and Carter were sitting in their office trying to figure what to put on TV next when a lady from eastern North Carolina stuck her head through the door and said she'd just come by to say hello.

Mr. Ellis reared back in his chair and said they were in a helluva mess that the Panama Canal had given out of gas and did she have any ideas.

What happened next is straight out of Club lore. That lady who'd never seen a poll had two ideas. She said the way she saw it tobacco farmers were hurting in the east and textile workers were hurting in the west and she wasn't Arthur Finkelstein but if it was up to her she'd put two ads on the air and tell them what John East meant to do about it –

which is exactly what Tom Ellis did and East won the Senate election by six thousand votes.

The other odd thing about Mr. Ellis and Arthur and Carter was how much they all hated bumper stickers. It was irrational. They'd raise twenty million dollars and they wouldn't buy a bumper sticker to put in the Moore County headquarters. It got so bad the volunteers running the county offices started secretly buying their own bumper stickers out of mail-order catalogues which I guess violated a dozen federal elections laws but there's only so many times you can tell a redneck who comes in the local Helms headquarters dead-set on putting a Jesse sticker on his pick-up truck, 'No. There aren't any.'

After Reagan won and East won and Gene Johnston won without pausing to take a breath The Club charged straight into the 1982 election.

Since Republicans controlled everything in Washington but the House of

Representatives they supported five candidates for Congress and tried a new weapon in their ads: Humor. In one race they made an ad with calypso music about Congressman Charlie Rose taking a junket to Rio de Janeiro with a female aide. They gave the ad to Rose's Democratic opponent in the primary and to the Republican in the General Election and about the worst thing that can happen to a politician happened to Charlie Rose – people started laughing about his 'Free-o to Rio.'

⌘

In Pinehurst a respected local businessman, Harris Blake, who'd built his own hardware business and building supply business from scratch decided to run for Congress.

Harris's office and mine were nestled in the same office park not more than a hundred yards apart and for the better part of a year I worked hand in glove with Carter building Harris's campaign – but in the end we ran head on into another of those elections where one party can't win and the other can't lose. It was 1974 all over again. Even the Democrats – hard as they tried – couldn't lose the 1992 election.

They barely stopped celebrating on election night when Jim Hunt threw his hat in the ring against Jesse Helms.

CHAPTER FOUR

The Difference Between Puritans and Cavaliers

Back in 1984 we Helms people had no doubt Jim Hunt had two horns and a tail. A few years later when Republicans had a majority in the state House, one night I climbed the stairs to the Governor's Mansion and stared at the door certain as soon as it swung open I was going to walk straight into Lucifer's den and come face to face with a villain capable of any wickedness.

Instead I came face to face with a teetotaling, high school English teacher's son who had a corny streak a mile wide that was just plain funny.

Once Hunt gave a speech at Columbia University on early childhood education and I lost my mind and went to New York along with Tony Rand to hear him. At lunch just before his speech, out of the blue, Hunt looked across the table and said, 'Carolyn and I went to a great play last night.' Now I figured he'd seen *Hamlet* or *Les Miserables* but in the next breath he said, 'It's called *The Twenty-Fifth Annual Putnam County Spelling Bee.*' That's what I mean by corny. Who else but Jim Hunt would go to New York to see a play about a spelling bee? He liked that play so much the next thing I knew it was playing at Memorial Auditorium in Raleigh.

Carolyn Hunt was a farm girl from Iowa whose husband had gotten tangled up in politics and she'd gone along like a good wife but, truth be told, she'd have been happier just to stay on their farm in Rock Ridge – and she did stay there a good part of Hunt's last two terms as governor. And Carolyn Hunt knew farming. One of the darnedest conversations I ever heard was Carolyn explaining to my wife, Cindy, how to artificially inseminate a cow.

Hunt was as tough a governor as I ever dealt with but right there alongside that toughness was an old-fashioned streak of bone-deep niceness – he drew his partisan lines in the sand but when he was done he'd shove politics aside and lean back and be pretty good company.

Jim Martin, by comparison, tended to be a bit aloof. In part I think that was because Jim was unusually intellectual for someone in politics. Jim would take a problem, look at it ten different ways, puzzle it out and decide what he wanted to do then he just wanted the legislature to get out of his way and let him do it. He was also just naturally a peacemaker but most times when he held out an olive branch to quarrelsome Democratic legislators it turned out to be a one way street, which gave him a jaundiced view of legislators.

Marc Basnight, the Democratic Senate Leader, was the polar opposite of Governor Martin. Marc took a jaundiced view of governors. Any governor. Democrat or Republican. One of Marc's convictions was any governor's goal in life was to run right over the legislature. And his mission in life was to stop them. Marc was about the only person in the legislature who could dive into a scrape with Jim Hunt and come out in one piece and more than a few Republicans liked him for it.

A lot of folks got the idea Governor Easley was odd. That was a mantra among Democrats in the legislature. But the fact is Governor Easley was just naturally cautious. He tended to hold other people at arm's length until he figured out whether or not to trust them. On the other hand, once Mike Easley decided to let his hair down he was a pistol. And he had a mean sense of humor.

Jim Black the Democratic House Speaker was a blue-ribbon mumbler and he just drove Governor Easley crazy – Easley'd be sitting in the Governor's Mansion and Black would be sitting not four feet away and Easley's head would jerk up and he'd light into Black, saying, *What's that? What's that you said? Stop that damn mumbling. You got a wad of chewing tobacco in your mouth or something?*

Black's mumbling got under the skin of Tony Rand the Democrats' floor leader in the Senate too – I think one reason Rand and I got along was he preferred an argumentative Republican to a Democratic mumbler.

Once I put in a local bill that affected only the Republican County Commissioners in my home county and it sailed through the House but when it got over to the Senate the Democrats held it up. The day it came up to a vote in Committee I went to the hearing and there was Tony Rand running the show. Right away a Democratic Senator, R.C. Soles, let fly hammer and tongs and you'd have thought I'd put in a bill to cut the public school budget.

Right in the middle of R.C.'s harangue I looked over at Tony and rolled my eyes as if to say, *Is all this posturing necessary?*

Tony leaned toward R.C. and drawled, 'R.C., you know this is a local bill that's about Republicans screwing Republicans.'

R.C. reared back and grinned. 'In that case, Mr. Chairman, I move we give it a favorable report.'

Now, compared to Democrats, Republican legislators could be just plain prickly. We're also proof there's always more of a tendency to fight when it's inside the family and the fight's meaner too. Some people say that's because being in a minority so long has just made Republican legislators more plain ornery than Democrats. Most times when you got three Republican legislators together in a room you had the makings of a fight on your hands.

And I've got a theory why.

We Republicans have inherited a streak of Puritanism. We've got our creed and on things like raising taxes we don't have much give in us. As Puritans we naturally see the world through one set of glasses and it's a short step from there to seeing Jim Hunt as a devil with two horns and a tail.

Democrats are more broad minded. As a result they get infected with all kinds of different creeds and ideas and a lot of times that means they have a hard time seeing what's just plain wrong – but on the other hand their being more tolerant of people who don't see things the way they do makes them a lot easier to get along with.

There was a Republican theorist who once traced Republicans Puritan streak back to the English Civil War in 1642. He said we Republicans had inherited our politics from Oliver Cromwell and the Roundheads while the Democrats were heirs to the more fun-loving Cavaliers.

⌘

Anyway, in 1984 Jim Hunt ran against Jesse and anyone who lived through it can tell you it was politics on a grand scale and pure hell at the same time.

Bill Friday once interviewed Tom Ellis on his TV show and in that academic way Bill had he asked, 'Tom, there are a lot of folks who accuse you of negative campaigning. How do you answer that?'

Mr. Ellis shot right back, 'Well, Bill, politics ain't kickball.'

Jesse and Jim Hunt both proved that in 1984.

The third genius at The Congressional Club, after Tom Ellis and Arthur Finkelstein, was Bob Harris. Bob was the only person at The Club who ended up getting profiled on *60 Minutes*. How that happened is odd because The Club avoided reporters like the plague and the last person you'd ever expect them to let inside their headquarters with a TV camera was Mike Wallace.

But the producer of Wallace's program heard about Bob from a mutual friend and flew down to Raleigh to meet him and the program he made wasn't about politics it was about raw courage.

The first time I met Bob he was confined to a wheelchair – not just confined he had to wear a special body brace to hold him up so he could sit in the chair. Bob had a rare disease – like multiple sclerosis – and when he graduated from North Carolina State University magna cum laude in three years Tom Ellis asked him to run The Club's research in the late 1970s. Around 1981 or 1982 his disease came out of remission and after he got out of the hospital he was confined to his bed. For two years he did every bit of the research in the Helms vs. Hunt campaign lying flat on his back and when he was done he knew more about Jim Hunt than Hunt knew about himself.

Jesse started out a whopping twenty-five points behind Hunt so The Club didn't waste any time. Over a year before the election they started running ads attacking Hunt and found out it was like chiseling granite. By the end of the year they'd chipped and whittled and hammered away and spent four or five million dollars but only gained six points. By December they were broke so just before Christmas they stopped running ads long enough to work on their fundraising to refill their coffers and, right then, when they wanted it least the Democratic Party slammed Jesse with its first two mean radio ads.

Arthur flew down to Raleigh toting a poll and announced if they didn't answer those ads they'd probably lose the six points that had just cost them five million dollars and nobody in that room felt like gambling.

Money was tight so instead of TV ads Bob Harris faxed over three scripts for radio ads. They were simple. All they said was: 'I'm Jesse Helms and I opposed the Panama Canal Giveaway. Where do you stand, Jim?' Then they repeated the same exact statement four more times but with a different issue each time.

Arthur took one look at those scripts and said, 'Why not just break these up into ten-second TV ads?' Which was even cheaper than radio.

The Club put those dinky little ten-second ads on TV and Jesse shot up in the polls – he gained six more points on Hunt in three weeks and The Club had found the key to beating Hunt: His flip-flops.

After that The Club's ads were simple and brutal. One ad showed a clip of Hunt saying how he supported longer school years to improve education; five seconds later another clip flashed up on the screen of Hunt saying – a year earlier – that he supported shorter school years. After they'd done that on about three different issues every time they asked, 'Where do *you* stand, Jim?' they had people laughing at Hunt.

By summer they'd caught Hunt in the polls and from there to the fall the race was a dead heat.

In October, Hunt hired Dick Morris – who had worked for Bill Clinton – to do a special poll which was going to tell Hunt how to whip Jesse. Morris flew down to Raleigh, settled into a chair in one of the high-ceilinged rooms in the Governor's Mansion, faced Governor Hunt and Carolyn Hunt and two dozen Hunt campaign brain-thrusters from everywhere from New York to eastern North Carolina and flipped open the poll and said they were running the campaign backwards.

He said all they had to do was look at their ads to see it. They were telling folks Jesse was a right-wing nut but everybody in North Carolina already knew that. Those ads weren't going to change a single vote. To win they had to tell voters something about Jesse they didn't know – like where he stood on abortion.

Morris closed the poll and said, 'That's the *only* ad I'd run.'

That set off one hell of a row. The Hunt folks split right down the middle and had a brawl with half of them wanting to tear into

Jesse on abortion and half not wanting to touch that polecat with a ten-foot pole.

They fought and argued until they were worn out then they did about the worst thing they could have – at the end of a campaign when the chips were on the table they equivocated. Instead of slamming Jesse between the eyes with a last-ditch TV ad on abortion they decided they'd stick their toes in the water and tweak him with a radio ad.

After the campaign, sitting on the deck behind my house looking out over the lake Carter told me what happened next: He was driving to The Club one morning when a nice sounding lady came on the radio and said sweetly, 'Did you know Jesse Helms is against abortion – even if a woman is raped?' The woman's voice took on a sharper edge. 'Do you know even if a woman is the victim of incest – Jesse Helms wants to make her have the baby?'

By then Carter was thinking Hunt had just given 90% of the women in North Carolina two good reasons to vote against Jesse then the high-sounding lady said, 'Jesse Helms even opposes the IUD and the birth control pill.'

Carter's first thought was, *I never thought I'd hear IUDs discussed on WPTF Radio.* His next thought was, *They went too far. They stretched the truth and blew the ad.*

The way Carter saw it no one was going to believe Jesse opposed the birth control pill. Even if Jesse had voted against abortion for rape and incest he hadn't voted against the pill and just saying it was plain ridiculous. Hunt had told such a whopping lie nobody was going to believe one word in that ad.

An hour later he was sitting at his desk when Tom Ellis roared through the door and said he'd just heard Hunt's radio ad and to get Bob on the phone and get Earl Ashe – who made the TV ads – into the office because he meant to have the answer to that Hunt ad on the air by dawn.

But the way Carter saw it that meant taking their ads off the air about Hunt's flip-flops – so the Helms folks just like the Hunt folks a few nights before went to having a row.

Tom Ellis shot back he wasn't so sure about people not believing Jesse opposed the birth control pill and right about then the phone rang and it was a lady who'd known Jesse thirty years and she said, *Tom, tell me that ad's not true.*

They went on arguing and just like the Hunt folks they guessed wrong. They ignored the ad until they got back a poll that said Jesse had dropped 20 points among women under 40 and as Carter said later it didn't need to be true about Jesse opposing the birth control pill – all those women had to do was get a whiff it might be and they weren't taking any chances.

The next morning around dawn Tom Ellis walked up the sidewalk to Jesse's house and rapped on the door and handed Dot Helms a script for a TV ad. An hour later Mrs.

Helms looked into a camera in a TV studio and said Jim Hunt had told an 'outright falsehood' and Jesse had never opposed the birth control pill – which was probably not something Dot Helms ever dreamed she'd say on television.

The Hunt folks took one look at Dot Helms TV ad and blinked a second time – they decided they'd had all they wanted of that fight and whipped their radio ad off the air.

Two decades later Carter Wrenn and Gary Pearce, who worked in Jim Hunt's campaign, still haven't found much to agree on but one thing they'll both tell you is pulling that ad may have cost Jim Hunt the election.

And that's one more lesson in politics: In most campaigns it's not what the other fellow does that beats you – it's what you do to beat yourself.

CHAPTER FIVE

A Whole New World of Sinning

When I ran for State House in 1990 my first problem wasn't Democrats it was local pachyderms.

Back then the pachyderms ran the Moore County party like a fiefdom. They hand-picked the candidates. They decided who should and shouldn't run. And what they decided in my case was I shouldn't even think about it.

When I announced it was like turning back the clock to the days of the Helms-Holshouser feud. George Little, my old business associate, had his own candidate running and Governor Holshouser, himself, was Chairman of my opponent's campaign.

Then, just to be sure I lost, the pachyderms recruited a third candidate – a spoiler – to run and split my vote in the rural northern end of Moore County, which had been Republican from the days of Lincoln when they hadn't wanted to secede.

The Club had its hands full with Harvey Gantt running against Jesse and didn't usually get into local elections but one night after dinner Carter said, 'Well, I reckon you're going to need some help dealing with George and those other lizards.'

'It looks like I am.'

Arthur did the polls, Bob did the research, Earl Ashe made the ads, Carter did the media, Mark Stephens all but ran the campaign and we broke all kinds of new ground. No one had ever heard of a local candidate taking a poll or running a TV ad. The way Carter put it our plan was simple, 'Here's how you win. There are fourteen thousand Republicans in Moore County and only a handful of pachyderms. You talk to the

Republicans and go around the pachyderms' – and that's what our ads did. We talked straight to those fourteen thousand voters and won the primary outright without a runoff.

Not that it wasn't testy. Governor Holshouser, whom I'd known for sixteen years, had a memory lapse in the middle of the election and told the local newspaper he couldn't remember me working in his administration. Gene Anderson who'd been the governor's chief political aide wrote a letter to the newspaper setting that straight. (In fact, I'd been the last person to leave Governor Holshouser's office, carrying the last box out to Gene's car the morning Jim Hunt was sworn in.)

The Democrats had a strong candidate in the General Election but Jesse was running at the top of the ticket and he was pretty popular in Moore County so we just melded my campaign in with his. He got 58% of the votes and I got 54%.

I was sworn into office on a cold raw January day in 1991 and found myself sitting right in the middle of a whole new world of sinners.

CHAPTER SIX
Lizards

When I got elected to the State House I crossed a line. In elections you deal with thousands of voters but in the House you deal with one hundred and twenty legislators.

Though I didn't know it the morning I saw down in the House Chamber, Robert Grady – the Representative from Jacksonville – had also been at Carolina the same time as Carter and I. Robert had worked in Reagan's campaigns with Carter, then he ran for House in 1984 and won – the first Republican elected from eastern North Carolina.

Art Pope was elected the same year I was. Art was from a prominent Raleigh family and his father, John Pope, was a businessman from the old school – he'd started out from scratch and pulled himself up by his bootstraps.

I gather Art had gotten bit by the political bug early. In high school he'd worked, I think, in Jack Hawke's campaign for Congress then when he graduated from law school he worked for Jack in Jim Martin's campaign for Governor.

Like his father, who was a close friend of Tom Ellis, Art's politics were straight down the line conservative. But not instinctive conservative – intellectual conservative. Hair thinning even in his early thirties, perennially disheveled, shirt wrinkled, shirt-tail half out, weaving down the halls of the legislature wearing a rumpled suit Art was by nature and inclination one of a rare breed of people who don't often run for public office: An old-fashioned policy wonk. The type of intellectual who could spend hours glued to a computer or wading through mounds of state budget documents or archaic regulations and when he was done there wasn't a bone buried in the budget Art hadn't dug up and chewed on.

Over the years he and his family would fund – personally – half a dozen think-tanks that Art would put to work studying everything from the North Carolina Constitution to the state regulations on well water.

His family gave so generously to the Republican Party – one newspaper put it at over $700,000 – in gratitude the party named the state headquarters 'The Pope Building.'

Art had an odd quirk when it came to the word no. He might take a 'no' intellectually – which was fine. Or he might take a no personally.

Once I told Art no – a few days later he walked into my office and rapped a list down on the middle of my desk of every candidate and group he and his family had given money to. Later, I thought it over and decided he'd given me that list for two reasons. First, a lot of the Republican legislators on that list had supported me in one way or the other – the way Art saw it he'd helped me and my telling him no was a kind of ingratitude on my part. Second, I think the way Art looked at that list it wasn't just names and dollar amounts. It was part of who he was. It was part of being Art Pope and when I told him no I might as well have said one of his virtues didn't amount to a hill of beans – so he took that no as a personal insult.

⌘

After Art served a single term in the legislature he decided to run for Lieutenant Governor and I supported him. He won the primary but lost in the general election.

The same year I had my second hard-fought primary and another tough general election and won.

That fall Leo Daughtry was also elected to the House from Johnston County. Leo looked like a candidate, tall, genial and soft-spoken with a rural southerners' drawl. An attorney, he'd served in the State Senate until the Democrats gerrymandered him out of his district then he'd switched and run for the House.

Later when I asked Carter about Leo he shrugged and said, 'Well, Leo's pachyderm pedigree goes way back.'

Back in 1972 the first time Jesse ran for Senate, Tom Ellis had some pretty definite ideas about who should lead Jesse's campaigns in the rural Democratic counties in eastern North Carolina and it wasn't Republican courthouse lawyers. He got two prominent Democrats to head Jesse's campaign in Leo's home county and six years later Mr. Ellis did it again – got Democrats to lead Jesse's campaign.

It wasn't easy being a Republican in a county where Democrats outnumbered Republicans five or six or seven to one and every time Leo and the other local pachyderms thought of those Democrats running Jesse's campaign it just stuck in their craw. The backbiting got so bad Carter had to go down there to meet with Leo and the Republican Party Chairman to straighten out the mess. When he came back he said, 'First, they're not particularly concerned about Jesse winning but they are concerned a lot about who gets the credit if he does. Second, Leo's a lizard.'

I once asked Carter, 'Define lizard.'

He lit a cigar. 'Well, a lizard is sort of like pornography. You know one when you see one.'

A lizard was about the worst thing the folks at The Club could call anyone. Lizards in their view were a race apart made up of the most untrustworthy people in politics. A lizard was a politician who'd risen above the usual sleight of hand either out of pure meanness or an absolute lack of scruples.

I don't think Leo was ambitious in the same way most politicians are. He didn't have a burning hunger to be a Governor or Senator – like Jim Hunt did. I think he'd have been content to sit in the House as genial old Leo Daughtry except part of him was like the fellow sitting in the Rotary Club who looks around one day and decides he might like to be President. In Leo's case he decided after his first term he ought to be Republican Leader.

His big problem was Representative Harold Brubaker from Asheboro. Harold had been in the House a lot longer than Leo and he'd already been Republican Leader once – so Leo set out to get Harold's support which didn't turn out to be a problem or, at least, not the kind of problem Leo expected. Leo asked Harold to endorse him and Harold looked Leo in the eye and proposed a swap: He said he'd support Leo for Republican Leader if Leo would support him for Speaker of the House.

Now no Republican had been elected Speaker of the House since 1896 and, right then, at the moment the Democrats had a whopping eighteen-seat majority in the House and there was no way on earth Republicans could pick up more than five or six seats – so to Leo that looked like a pretty good swap. He'd get Harold's support for Republican

Leader in exchange for supporting Harold for an office Harold couldn't win.

Only lightning struck. The 1994 election turned out to be one of those once in a decade debacles – like 1974 or 1982 – when a tidal wave roared across the state that swept one party into office – only this time it was the Republicans. It was blind dumb luck but Harold had outsmarted Leo – when the votes were counted Republicans had picked up twenty-six seats and had an eight-seat majority.

Which left Leo in a dilemma because he'd set out to be top Republican in the House and he didn't see himself playing second fiddle to Harold as Speaker.

Leo and Harold had the same political consultant, Paul Shumaker, who'd worked in Governor Martin's campaigns. Before the caucus Leo got Paul to set up a meeting with Harold, just the three of them sitting around a table, with Leo looking for a loophole to get out of his promise and Harold just sitting there not blinking, refusing to budge.

In the middle of the meeting Harold got up and left the room for five minutes and as soon as he disappeared out the door – the way Paul tells it – Leo leaned to Paul and snapped, *Alright, tell me how to get this turkey out of the race?*

Paul thought about that a minute. *Well, it looks to me like it all comes down to whether or not you mean to keep your word.*

Paul wasn't exactly right. What it probably boiled down to was whether or not Leo could get enough votes in the Republican Caucus to beat Harold. There are some politicians who'll bet the house against the odds but Leo wasn't one of them. He weighed the risk of running for Speaker and losing, then studied the sure thing of being Majority Leader and just that little bit of doubt made up his mind.

⌘

After Harold was elected Speaker he appointed me Chairman of the Rules Committee which put me squarely in line for a head butting of my own with Leo because of House Rule 36-A – a rule that said when a bill came out of a House committee the only way it could get to the floor for a vote was if I (as Rules Chairman) put it on the calendar; which meant if Harold didn't want a bill passed he'd say, 'Richard, hold it up,' then I'd get to look every legislator – including Leo – dead set on passing his bill in the eye and say 'No.'

I'll tell you something I've never figured out: How to tell a legislator 'No' without making him mad. That's a trick Houdini couldn't have pulled off. I tried blunt. I tried nice. I tried hard. I tried smooth. Nothing made any difference. In the end blunt worked simplest so I just settled for blunt but I'll tell you one other thing: If you want to win the Mr. Congeniality award in the State House don't serve as Rules Committee Chairman.

⌘

The other thing that happened after Republicans won the majority was Art – who'd been out of the House since he'd run for Lt. Governor – resurfaced and decided he wanted to be Harold's Chief of Staff. Then Art decided he ought to be Harold's Legal Counsel too. By then he was skating on thin ice but he didn't seem to mind because next he started laying down conditions: Telling Harold if he was going to be Chief of Staff he should have control over writing the state budget.

Now there are some things only a legislator can do and Harold figured out pretty quickly not one of the sixty-eight Republicans in the House were going to sit still for Art handing them a budget and saying, *There it is. Pass it.*

The ice cracked under Art's feet and Harold washed his hands of the whole mess and put Alan Pugh and Tripp Sizemore in charge of his staff.

Next Art decided to run for a seat on the University of North Carolina Board of

Governors and asked me to support him and I did.

The Board runs the universities and the legislature elects the members so all Art had to do was get the House Republicans to vote for him. The problem was, after he'd suggested he ought to write the state budget, a lot of legislators – including Harold – had decided he'd gotten too big for his britches. He ran and lost and it was the straw that broke the camel's back.

Looking back, I think, what happened next had a lot to do with that list of donations Art once showed me – because, after all, if he was keeping lists of how much money The Pope Family gave to Republicans he was probably keeping lists of the money they gave the university too – which meant the House Republicans voting against him was a double insult. Because they'd said as far as they were concerned Art's lists didn't matter a toot.

What they missed was it mattered a lot to Art and human nature being what it is after

Art lost that vote it was only a matter of time before the pot boiled over. The two people he blamed most were Harold and Harold's political consultant, Paul Shumaker. I'd say hate is not too strong a word for how Art felt about Paul. Naturally, he didn't like being sandbagged by Harold one bit but being sandbagged by what he saw as Harold's two-bit political consultant had to be just plain galling.

I'd supported Art for Chief of Staff and Legal Counsel and for the Board of Governors but in a blood feud between politicians there are no neutrals. When Art looked at the House Republicans I was sitting in the pew right beside Harold and I was about to find out to my surprise beneath his rumpled suits Art had a mean streak.

⌘

Two years before, during the 1994 election, The Club had supported Chuck Neely, one of Tom Ellis' law partners for the House. During the campaign just like they'd done for me, they took polls and made ads – only this time Jack Hawke, the Republican Party Chairman, sent copies of the ads to Republican candidates all across the state, saying to use them in their campaigns – that all they had to do was change the names.

Chuck must have felt a lot of people got a free ride at his expense – since he paid for the ads – but in the end it worked out just fine for everyone. For the first time Republicans were running a statewide campaign for the House with Republican candidates everywhere talking about issues that came straight out of The Club's polls – like the Democrats voting themselves a pay raise.

I set out to repeat that in 1996. To run a statewide campaign.

Carter was in New Jersey with Steve Forbes' presidential race so I recruited Mark Stephens and Calvin Kervin and Bob Rosser, who'd all worked for The Club, and Paul Shumaker to build the campaign.

That fall we won the election and the second Republican majority took office in 1997.

Then Carter decided to run ads attacking Republican legislators.

CHAPTER SEVEN

Sharks' Fins in the Water

Of all the things two people ever had a falling out over, I guess hog farm regulations is one of the dumbest. Carter and I proved we both had a streak of just plain foolishness or maybe it was stubbornness.

In the 1990's hog farming became a multi-billion dollar business in North Carolina – it was growing and mushrooming and a lot of people were concerned about the threat to the environment so the legislature passed a 'moratorium' which put a freeze on opening new farms.

The hog farmers reaction was simple: They decided it was time to get active in politics and since most of them supported

Jesse and had been members of The Congressional Club they already knew Carter.

One night after the House adjourned Carter and I had dinner to try to straighten out the mess but, instead, neither of us gave an inch and when he said, 'Richard, this is not a fight you want,' it sounded like a threat to me – after that common sense went right out the window.

Carter made "issue ads" for the farmers, attacking four Republican legislators then a group of Republican legislators – including me – filed a complaint with the Board of Elections because the ads were illegal and the whole thing erupted. Carter turned the Elections Board hearing into a political brawl and let Harold have it with both barrels – after that we were both mad enough no one stopped to take a breath or look back.

The fight took on a life of its own. Lawyers piled in on both sides and the hearing in the Elections Board boiled over into a fight that roared out of the Board to the Wake

County District Attorney then to the Federal Court in Raleigh then to the Federal Circuit Court in Richmond where three federal judges said no matter what North Carolina election law said about issues ads they were legal.

The other problem in 1997 was with Leo and Art.

During the Elections Board hearing a lot of charges were hurled at Harold and the Board started investigating and the newspapers cranked up and rumors started flying Harold was about to get indicted and in a flash Art's fin was in the water circling like a shark. Art started calling legislators, saying he was taking the delegation's pulse and, by the way, if Harold got indicted how did they feel about supporting Leo for Speaker?

When the Board exonerated Harold, Art's fin disappeared and Leo's popped up.

The problem started with 'Tort Reform.'

Tort Reform was one of the bills in the 'House Contract' every Republican – including Leo – had signed. But it was stuck in a committee Leo chaired going nowhere. One morning Leo called and asked if I could come over to his office and when I walked through the door Dick Taylor the chief lobbyist for the Trial Lawyers Association was waiting.

The trial lawyers have one of the biggest political action committees in North Carolina; they spend hundreds of thousands of dollars each year to elect their allies and they're one of the pillars of the State Democratic Party. Election after election they had almost exclusively supported Democrats but when Republicans won the majority, naturally, they started looking for friends on our side of the aisle and they found Leo.

I looked at Leo, looked at George Holmes, the other Republican Legislator in the room, and nodded at Dick and Leo drawled, 'Dick and I've been talking and we're thinking this might be a good time to start some new friendships.'

But 'friendship' wasn't exactly what Leo had in mind.

Dick could be pretty blunt and straightforward – he didn't try to gild the lily and I didn't either. I said friendships sounded fine but last election he'd tried to whip me and just about every other Republican in the House and the blunt fact was we were dead-set on passing Tort Reform and he was dead-set on stopping it so where exactly did he see our common ground?

Leo started to fidget, decided to play peace-maker and then I laid the real polecat on the table. 'Leo, I reckon you've just taken a wad of money from the trial lawyers and now you've called this meeting because you're worried about how much heat you're going to get from me and the other Republicans and the answer is plenty.'

Because any way I looked at it the Republican Chairman of the committee that was supposed to pass Tort Reform taking money from the trial lawyers was going to smell pretty bad.

In fact it got to smelling so bad after chewing it over Leo decided to send the money back.

Which solved one problem but aggravated another.

When the House Republicans passed a bill it would sail over to the Senate and the Senate Democrats had three choices: Pass it, change it, or kill it. What would happen next wasn't quite as crude as horse trading but the two have a lot in common.

One of Leo's jobs, as Majority Leader, was to sit in backrooms negotiating with Democratic Senators, trying to get them to pass our bills. The problem boiled over when a group of Republican legislators got the idea what Leo was really doing was trading away their bills to get the Democrats to pass bills he favored.

When Leo started playing footsie with the trial lawyers a lot of Republican legislators decided it was time they started doing their own negotiating. And how they went about it was simple. They started asking me – as Rules Committee Chairman – to stop the bills Democratic Senators sent over to the House.

The Democratic Senators got the message and started trooping over to the House asking me to bring their bills to a vote then I'd name a Republican legislator – say, for instance, Wilma Sherrill – and say, 'Well, you're blocking Wilma's bill over in the Senate so why don't the two of you get together and work out your differences and when you do whatever Wilma decides is fine with me.'

That made most House Republican legislators happy – but Leo.

CHAPTER EIGHT

You Lie and I'll Endorse You

When Senator Lauch Faircloth was beaten by John Edwards in 1998 the ripples washed straight down through the House elections and we lost our majority.

And the Jim Black era began.

At first glance you wouldn't have taken Jim for any kind of politician at all. Most everything he did was slow. He walked slow, talked slow and hardly ever got excited. He'd shuffle down House hallways stoop-shouldered, amble into a meeting room and slouch down in a chair and start mumbling under his breath.

But people didn't make the mistake of underestimating Jim but once.

He'd become Democratic leader back in 1995 after the Democrats lost their first election. Until then they'd been defeating Republican candidates year in and year out for a century – no one could even remember a close election. Then, suddenly, they had to start running campaigns. Only they had no idea how. They'd hardly ever taken a poll or made a TV ad.

Jim Black was about to change that single-handedly.

But, first, he ran head on into another problem: Money. During the years when Democrats had been in power whenever they needed money they'd hold a fundraiser and a legion of Raleigh lobbyists would flock down to the Legislature bearing checks – but the first time Jim ran up the distress flag after losing the majority hardly a single lobbyist showed up. He found himself staring a blunt truth straight in the eyes: No majority, no money.

So he set out to change that too and over the next four years he did but along the way he planted a lot of poisonous seeds that were going to come back to haunt him.

Back then video poker was a big business in North Carolina but the sheriffs were dead-set against it. When they asked the legislature to ban it Marc Basnight didn't have to think twice. He whipped a bill through the Senate then the video poker operators needed friends over in the House.

They already had one in Leo who'd been representing them in court for years – once the Sheriff of Randolph County had told me how he arrested a video poker operator for illegal gambling and the operator hired Leo, who kept postponing the trial while the legislature was in session.

But the first time I tried to pass a bill to ban video poker the problem I ran into wasn't Leo – it was Jim Black.

A lot's been said critical of Jim and the 'pay to play' scandals that came later. But, to give him credit, in 1998 he single-handedly dragged the House Democrats into the Twentieth Century politically and it's hard for me to see how they would have won the election without him.

Unfortunately, eventually, he was going to learn winning can be as treacherous as losing.

⌘

Even before we lost the election Leo and Art had been talking about Leo replacing Harold as Speaker – but Jim Black had taken care of that for them. Next, before the House convened, Harold announced he wouldn't run for Republican Minority Leader either – then the caucus promptly split into equal factions.

I thought I would beat Leo by one vote: Instead, he beat me by one vote – only it turned out Leo didn't really want to be Republican Leader. He wanted to be Governor and he was using the House Leadership as a spring board to launch his campaign.

What happened next was pure Leo.

Leo and I had a mutual friend, Robert Holding, a businessman who placed the Club's TV and radio buys. One morning Robert called and asked if I'd sit down with him and Leo – the three of us met at my condominium in Raleigh, me sitting on the corner of the sofa, Leo in a chair facing me and Robert beside Leo. Leo didn't waste any time beating around the bush.

He handed me a piece of paper with ten statements – quotes – typed on it and said since he was running for governor he was going to resign as Republican Leader. Then he laid the deal he wanted to make on the table: He'd support me for Leader if I'd make one of those ten statements.

I read the list. What each statement said in a different way was Leo had the character and integrity to be governor. He was offering to swap me his endorsement for my lie and I don't believe it ever crossed his mind there was one thing wrong with that. That was just politics.

I laid the list on the table. 'Leo, I don't believe I can make even one of those statements.'

⌘

Leo may not just have been trying to swap for my endorsement – he may also have been double-crossing Art.

The legislator in Art's district had resigned and the local Republican Committee had picked Art to fill the seat – so he was back in the House for the first time in seven years and he was the other candidate running for Republican Leader.

When the caucus met I defeated Art by nine or ten votes – but in the long run Art turned out to be a lot worse enemy than Leo. Leo didn't really like to fight. He preferred to slip around the edges then make a deal. But Art was like a bull terrier. He charged right at you and if he got knocked down he'd jump right back up and charge again. And that's what he did after he lost the race for

Republican Leader. He made a good, old-fashioned, brass-knuckled power play.

Art came to my office, sat down and suggested I dump Julia Howard, the Republican Whip, and replace her with his candidate, Lanier Cansler, to unite the caucus.

I saw two problems: Art wasn't going to turn over a new leaf because Lanier became Whip. In his eyes this wasn't just a political fight it was a vendetta. More than his political enemy he saw me as his personal enemy. Second, Julia had won a vote in the caucus fair and square and their was no reason to replace her. Art's only real objection to Julia was she had supported me and not him in the caucus.

I looked back at him across the desk. 'That's it? You want me to double-cross Julia Howard? I can't do that.'

In politics women are a lot more direct than men. They don't tend to maneuver in the back rooms. When a woman has something on her mind most times she just comes out and says it. Julia was no wilting violet. When I told her what Art had proposed she went straight to Art and asked him if it was true and he looked her straight in the eye and said no.

Julia didn't beat around the bush. She more or less grabbed Art by the collar, led him down the hallway to my office, sat down, glared at me and said, 'Now, I'm going to get to the bottom of this.'

Art looked straight at me and denied it again. He said he'd never proposed I replace Julia with Lanier. I said:

'That's a lie and you know it.'

Art got mad, stood up, walked toward the doorway, stopped and looked back at me.

'I guess it's time to pick a side and go for blood.'

He was as good as his word.

⌘

Leo lost his primary for governor which left him with a knotty problem.

Once in Texas Lyndon Johnson ran once for two offices at the same time – for Vice President with John Kennedy and for a third term for Senate. That way if he lost the Vice Presidential race he could remain in the Senate.

Leo couldn't do that so after he lost his primary for Governor in May he wouldn't be returning to the House after the election that fall. Because he wasn't on the ballot. Another candidate had won the nomination for his House seat. But it turned out Leo had hand-picked the candidate who was running for his seat and he just told her to resign as the Republican nominee and in a flash he had the local Republican Committee pick him to take her place.

CHAPTER NINE

A Worse Enemy Than Leo

When the House convened for the short session in the summer of 2000 my biggest problem wasn't Art – it was figuring out how to raise the money to beat Jim Black and the Democrats in the fall election. By then I'd already been to Washington twice with Bill Cobey, the Republican State Chairman, to ask the National Party to help but we'd been turned down flat.

The hardest job in politics is raising money and I was relearning an old story: There are a lot of people who will talk about raising money, offer to raise money and promise to raise money but in the end it winds up just being talk. If you're going to raise a million dollars you'd better plan to do it yourself.

I sent Curt Anderson, who did polling for the caucus, back to Washington with a third proposal. I offered to contribute $100,000 from my own campaign to jumpstart our fundraising and challenged the National Party to do the same thing. To match my contribution.

Then I called a caucus of Republican legislators to discuss the campaign.

The day the caucus met Art invited Representatives Robert Grady and Edgar Starnes to dinner in a pub in downtown Raleigh and told them that night he was going to call for a vote of no confidence in me. Then he explained that he didn't need Robert or Edgar's support – he already had the votes to win. But, as a courtesy, he wanted them to know what was going to happen.

That may sound thoughtful. But it wasn't. In the language of politics it wasn't courtesy it was a warning. Art was telling

Robert and Edgar: I have the votes. I don't expect you to support me. But for your own good, maybe you ought not to show up at the caucus tonight.

⌘

I opened the caucus with a report on our fundraising and the key districts Mark Stephens and Paul Shumaker said we had to win, glanced toward Robert and Edgar, then sat back to wait for the explosion.

It didn't come – at least not right away.

Art had asked Representative Carolyn Russell to make his motion but, right there, as she was sitting in the meeting Carolyn changed her mind.

That slowed Art down but it didn't stop him.

He scrambled around the room whispering to legislators until he finally got Representative Lyons Gray to agree to make the motion.

Only Lyons threw Art a curveball. He didn't make it right away.

Instead Art's allies started making speeches and the more they talked the madder they got and the meaner they got. Lyons sat there listening to all that venom until he'd heard enough then stood up, looked at Art and in front of the whole room said, 'I can't in good conscience make that motion.'

Art just picked himself up and charged again.

One thing you can always get a group of legislators stirred up about is money. Art stood up and made a motion to get control of the money we were spending to elect our candidates that fall out of my hands. He proposed the caucus vote to set up a Special Campaign Oversight Committee and Leo, sitting on the front row, piped up, 'I second that motion.'

Then Art made another motion. He demanded the caucus set up an Audit Committee headed by his ally Lanier Cansler and that came pretty close to saying outright I'd jiggered the money.

At first I started to get mad then I thought, *What difference does it make?* An audit didn't matter because every penny the caucus spent was already reported to the State Board of Elections where every newspaper in the state could see it – so there were no secrets. One more audit wouldn't matter.

And as far as Art controlling how we spent money that fall the simple fact was the caucus campaign committee operated under the umbrella of the State Party. Each check had to be approved by the State Chairman, Bill Cobey, and no matter what Art's new Committee said Bill and I both had to sign off on the checks. I said, 'Fine. Audit away,' and adjourned the caucus.

⌘

Before the caucus both the Republican and Democratic Campaign Committees had filed finance reports and there'd been a bombshell in Jim Black's report. Jim had personally loaned his campaign a staggering

$500,000 – more money than we'd raised all year.

Seven years later a State Board of Elections auditor going through a stack of Jim Black's financial statements turned up a fact a battalion of FBI agents and U.S. Attorneys had missed – a $500,000 check written to Jim Black by one of Raleigh's biggest lobbyists, just before Black filed his report. The lobbyist had loaned Jim $500,000. Then Jim turned around and loaned $500,000 to his campaign – so on that report he filed before the 2000 election it looked like he was awash in cash.

Then Jim pulled a reverse flim-flam. He took the $500,000 back, repaid himself, then repaid the lobbyist – but no one knew it because he didn't have to file another report for months.

But in a way Black out-smarted himself.

It was after I saw his report that I sent Curt Anderson to Washington with my offer to contribute $100,000 if the Republican Party would match it and this time the answer came back, Yes. A week later I found myself sitting in a car driving to Washington carrying a $100,000 check, with Mark Stephens – who I think just went along to be absolutely sure I didn't change my mind – sitting beside me.

That $200,000 jumpstarted our campaign. Before the election we raised $1.2 million and picked up four seats. Unfortunately that wasn't enough to replace Jim Black as Speaker. We were three seats shy of a majority. But those four seats we gained set the stage for everything that happened two years later.

CHAPTER TEN

Choices Between Evils

I remember once a fellow asked Jesse to run for some office or serve on some Senate committee and Jesse told him, *Well, if it wasn't for the honor of the thing I'd as soon pass.* After fighting with Art and Leo on one hand and Jim Black and the Democrats on the other I was beginning to feel the same way about running again for Republican Leader.

After the election when Harold invited a group of legislators to his home in Asheboro I told them about the last thing on earth I wanted to do was run again. I'd led three straight statewide campaigns – in 1996, 1998 and 2000 – for the caucus and raising that last million dollars was enough politics to hold me for a while – I was going to go home and sleep for a month.

They decided to support Joe Kiser.

Joe was a pretty unusual legislator. He'd been a sheriff and a teacher and a coach and along the way he'd learned a pretty uncommon lesson – Joe knew how to get along with almost everyone. After serving six years in a House with two Republican factions at each other's throats he hadn't made one enemy I knew of.

He ran and if he'd won he'd have been in line to be Speaker when Republicans retook the majority two years later – but Leo beat him by three votes.

I spent the next two years not fighting with anyone – then we won the 2002 election by a whisper. When the smoke cleared we had a one vote majority. And I was facing a choice – because my one vote could elect Leo Daughtry.

⌘

After the election Leo didn't waste any time. He hadn't made Harold any promises not to run for Speaker this time so with barely a blink he launched his campaign to get the caucus nomination.

The morning I drove up to Greensboro for the caucus I still didn't know what I was going to do but when I walked through the double doors of the hotel I had one fact clearly in focus. Sixty-one Republican votes would elect Leo Speaker – but sixty votes wouldn't elect him to anything.

Leo had the tracks greased. A lobbyist, Tommy Harrelson, who'd been Secretary of Transportation under Governor Martin hosted a buffet luncheon for legislators. I sat down at a round table at the back of the room, listened to ice clinking at the bar and glanced at the long whiteboard running along the wall.

After lunch they closed the doors but instead of Tommy leaving he walked to the wooden podium at the front of the room and started giving a speech – which struck me as odd. Why was a lobbyist speaking to the Republican Caucus? It turned odder. Like Leo, Tommy's pachyderm credentials went way back. Abraham Lincoln is the father of the Republican Party but that day Tommy waxed so eloquent he meant to give Lincoln a run for his money. He gave us the pachyderm version of the history of the Grand Old Party – at least in North Carolina – and listening to it was like Tommy and Leo had sweated and bled and toiled through it all. He talked about all the lean and barren years laboring in the Republican vineyards, then he talked about all the conventions he'd seen and the divisions and all the Republican blood he'd seen shed then he got right down to brass tacks: The one thing that mattered – with a one-vote majority – was the caucus staying united and what he meant was united behind Leo.

Tommy sat down and they held the first vote: The vote for Republican Majority Leader and Joe Kiser won hands down.

Then they opened the floor for nominations for Speaker. Leo was nominated and Connie Wilson from Charlotte was nominated. Then Harold stood up to speak and a legislator sitting at a table at the front of the room – who supported Leo – made it clear party unity didn't include Harold having his say. He cut Harold off and 'called the question' which is parliamentary maneuver to end debate and go straight to a vote.

We held the first ballot and Leo needed thirty-one votes to win and he got thirty-six and I started thinking a lot harder about the sixty-one votes he needed to be Speaker and almost missed what happened next.

The last vote was to pick the Republican nominee for Speaker Pro Tempore – the number two office in the House.

Michael Decker from Forsyth County and Joanie Bowie were nominated. The minute Joanie won Decker stood up, livid, face-flushed and glared at Leo then turned on his heel and stalked toward the door – as he passed my table he growled loud enough for everyone that side of the room to hear, *He did it to me again.*

Decker was a peculiar fellow. One year, I think his first year in the legislature, he slept in his office, taking sponge baths in the House bathroom. Later, he bought a van and lived out of it when he was in Raleigh.

Before he was elected he'd been a hard-shell fundamentalist, teaching history at *The Gospel Light Christian School.* Once, on the floor of the House, he'd come up to me and chewed me out for not voting for an amendment he'd sponsored opposing abortion – only he had it backwards. I'd voted for his bill and he'd confused me with another legislator. So I knew two things about Decker: He was – to put it the kindest way possible – eccentric and he had a temper.

After he stormed out the door the meeting meandered on; just before it ended I made up my mind, rose, walked out into the lobby of the hotel and stopped face to face with a line of reporters and TV cameras.

Art will tell you – and I think he means it in all sincerity – that supporting the caucus nominee's is, for a Republican legislator, pretty close to sacred obligation. It's part of that old Puritan mentality. You can't be a good Christian if you don't follow the teachings of your church; you can't be a good Republican if you don't follow the party line. I believe Art has confused religion and politics. I'd say when a man's party and his conscience are telling him two different things he ought not to confuse his party with the gospel. Boiled down to the bare bones the choice I had to make – after Leo was nominated – wasn't complicated at all.

Four years before Leo had offered me a simple swap: He would support me for Republican Leader if I would make a statement saying he should be governor and I'd told him no. Now thirty-six Republican legislators had decided he should be Speaker and Art wanted me to march in lockstep with them. But nothing had changed. Leo hadn't changed. Leo was still making deals. He'd just made – though I didn't know it then – and broken one with Michael Decker.

In politics there are days you only have choices between evils and a lot of sinning comes of those choices. But that day at the Republican caucus I had a third choice. It was like taking a long walk on a dark night on a short pier but I took a deep breath and looked into the TV cameras.

'I've decided to run for Speaker.'

CHAPTER ELEVEN

An Errant Gene

The first question came back like a pistol shot.

'Have you talked to Jim Black?'

Numbers have a wonderful clarity and like tyrants for the next two months two numbers marched across the hours and minutes and days: Sixty-one Republicans and fifty-nine Democrats.

I had spoken the words logic said meant sixty Republicans could never elect Leo Speaker – but that didn't mean he couldn't win. All he had to do was get one Democrat to vote for him and I had no doubt he could do that – by swapping a Committee

Chairmanship for a vote – before I could drive home to the farm.

Which led to my next problem: My one vote was not enough to stop Leo.

⌘

Hardly anything has ever come easy for Wilma Sherrill. She's been through hard times when just about all she could do was keep her head down and hold on and not give up until she saw a light at the end of the tunnel. When she called the morning after the caucus she didn't mince words.

'Well, I guess this makes me as big a fool as you are but from now on we're in this boat together.'

A man alone is prey to doubt and fear and lives a step ahead of despair but give him one companion and he'll ride off in search of the source of the Nile without a fear.

It was only going to take Leo a couple of minutes longer to trade for two Democratic votes rather than one – but that unexpected blessing phone call from Wilma Sherrill was the end of my doubts.

Danny McComas called next and offered to nominate me. Then I started calling legislators, first Harold, then Julia and, suddenly, I had five, then eight, then ten, then twelve votes – slowly but surely, the caucus began to unravel.

By the first of the year, instead of one Leo needed a dozen Democratic votes to win – only he didn't know it. That secret – how many Republicans were voting for me – was my only advantage. It meant if Leo guessed wrong and only swapped for two or three Democratic votes his deal would backfire.

Then a week before the House convened the unexpected happened.

Mike Decker lit a match and threw it on a powder keg.

It turned out that before the caucus in Greensboro Leo had made a deal with Decker: Decker would vote for Leo for Speaker, then Leo would support Decker for Speaker Pro

Tempore. And Decker did vote for Leo but then Leo double-crossed him and supported Joanie Bowie.

After the vote Decker got mad stayed mad and his temper was going to land him into a world of grief he never dreamed of.

It turned out after Mike Decker stalked out of the caucus growling, *He did it to me again*, he'd spent a week fuming and brooding and this time instead of Leo whispering in his ear – it was Jim Black.

Jim waited until a week before the House convened and dropped the bombshell: Decker had switched parties.

Anyway I looked at that it didn't make sense. A right-wing fundamentalist Christian changing parties to join arms with a caucus full of liberal Democrats. It looked to me like Decker had gotten mad and stayed mad until all that rage boiled over into blind revenge – because the simple fact was if all he wanted to do was stop Leo he'd miscalculated. He didn't need to change parties to do that. He could have done that by voting for me. Or, more simply, for himself.

It was going to be three years, until the morning Michael Decker walked into a federal courtroom and faced a judge, before I found the missing piece to that puzzle.

⌘

If it was revenge Decker wanted he got it. Before he switched there were Democrats who were ready to support Leo. The way they saw it was simple: Since Democrats only had a minority in the House voting for a Republican was not treachery. In fact almost every Republican legislator had voted for Jim Black for Speaker back in 2001 when Republicans were in the minority.

But after Decker's switch there were sixty Democrats and sixty Republicans in the House and the minute Democrats had an equal claim to the Speakership they stepped back and took a second look at the Speaker's race and decided electing Leo didn't look so good.

Suddenly, the man closest to being elected was Jim Black – who only needed one Republican vote to win.

And Jim set out to get it and he had a big advantage. He could trade with everyone: with Leo, with me, with any one single Republican legislator who'd vote for him and he could play all of us against each other.

All he had to do was put his sixty votes on the table and say, *Now, who wants to make me the best offer?*

Leo's position was weaker than Black's. He could horse trade with Black or go on trying to find a block of Democrats who'd break with Black to make a deal with him.

I had just one choice.

I had to deal with Jim Black. With just twelve votes, even if I got the support of a handful of Democrats I would lose.

And the first time I met with Black I learned I had an even worse problem.

When I met with Jim and Joe Hackney, the Democratic floor leader, and Bill

Culpepper, the Democratic Rules Committee Chairman, the first time at a restaurant in Raleigh, Jim's question was simple: Would I vote to make him Speaker. And my answer was no.

I told him with sixty Democrats and sixty Republicans in the House the only fair solution was to share power.

One interesting thing I've learned about negotiations is most times it's not what is said that matters – it's what no one needs to say.

Black's answer was polite but beneath his amicability were the words he didn't need – or bother – to say, *I can make that deal with Leo and unless that's what you want me to do you'd better make me a better offer.*

I leaned back and watched Black across the table and said, 'Jim, I believe I've gone about as far as I care to go.'

After that a deal with me was the last thing he wanted.

⌘

The deal he really wanted – and was moving heaven and earth to find – was to get one Republican to break ranks and vote for him and the way I saw it he had two good chances: Steve Wood and Cary Allred.

Steve had once made a deal with the Democrats back when Harold was Speaker. When Republicans nominated Carolyn Russell for Speaker Pro Tempore, Steve stood up on the House floor and, out of a clear blue sky, nominated himself – not more than two or three Republicans voted for him but every Democrat did and he won.

Cary Allred was the Republican Caucus resident maverick. At times it looked like just because everyone else was marching in one direction Cary, without logic or reason, would up and charge the other way just as fast and hard as he could. One moment he'd be careening in one direction and, the next, for no visible reason he'd change directions and careen the other way. It was like he had a malfunctioning gene that fired an impulse into his brain every minute or so that said whatever way he was marching was wrong and to reverse course.

His nickname, appropriately enough, was *Old Reliable*.

⌘

Leo never did like a fight and after Decker switched he was in a lot tougher fight than he'd expected and true to form he waited until the day before the House convened and tried to make a deal. It sounded like a sacrifice but in fact it wasn't.

Leo called a press conference and announced he was withdrawing from the Speaker's race in favor of a candidate who could unite the Republicans, then announced he was throwing his support to George Holmes. It's a mystery to me why Leo thought that would fool anyone. George was Leo's cat's-paw. George would be Speaker in name only while, behind the scenes, Leo would be the one running the House.

⌘

On opening day I sat down in the House Chamber and listened to the clerk call the roll. The vote was:

Jim Black – 60 votes

George Holmes – 55 votes

Richard Morgan – 5 votes

We were deadlocked.

We held four more votes. No one budged. No one changed.

One thing North Carolina legislators can do second to no one on earth is spread a rumor. The rumor sailed across the House floor after the fifth vote that the errant gene in Old Reliable's brain had fired and he was about to vote for Black – because Black had told him if he was elected he'd let Cary appoint twenty Committee Chairmen.

Joe Kiser scrambled to his feet and did the only thing he could. He made a motion to recess – which was the last thing on earth Black wanted because he had to get 'Old Reliable' to cast that vote before that errant gene fired again.

Every single Democrat voted against Joe's motion and it failed but before the clerk could begin to call the roll again Representative Edgar Starnes – a Republican – stood up in the back of the room and said he wanted to adjourn.

Now, practically, there's hardly any difference between a recess and an adjournment but under the rules of parliamentary procedure they're two different things and Edgar was entitled to a vote.

Legislators pressed the little red or green buttons on the front of their desks and the clerk threw a switch and the results flashed up on a black electronic panel – like a scoreboard at a high school basketball game – and whether it was chance, fate or simple human error the result was a minor miracle: One Democrat, Mary McAllister, pressed the wrong button and the Speakership, within Black's grasp, slipped through his fingers.

The House adjourned.

CHAPTER TWELVE

Three Deals and a Curveball

Black barely missed a beat. He had the deal he wanted with 'Old Reliable' but he decided to take out an insurance policy with Leo.

That night Jim and Joe Hackney and Bill Culpepper trooped over to the offices of Mutual Distributing Company, the beer and wine wholesaler Leo owned in Raleigh, and sat down face to face with Leo and George Holmes and Representative Ed McMahan.

Leo had been hoping he'd get Democratic Rep. Martin Nesbitt and a handful of Democrats to break ranks with Black and vote for him but he'd run into a stone wall.

What he was about to run into with Black was a buzzsaw.

The deal Jim threw on the table was the exact same offer he'd made to me only in reverse: Black could make a deal with me to share power and unless Leo wanted him to do it Leo'd better make a better offer.

Leo contemplated his future with me as Co-Speaker.

Carefully weighed his future with Black as Speaker alone.

And made Black the offer.

So Jim Black had three deals in his pocket. The one with 'Old Reliable' he wanted. One with Leo as an insurance policy. And one with me he didn't want – all he had to do was figure out how to juggle them.

He wanted the first vote the next morning to be on his deal with Cary so he threw Leo a curveball. He said he could live with the deal Leo had proposed but before he made a final commitment he'd have to run it by his caucus.

⌘

Later that night – at least I think it was that night, it may have been the next night – I got a telephone call from Bill Cobey, the Republican Party Chairman. I figured as Party Chairman he was making a more or less obligatory call to urge me to close ranks with the caucus and vote for Leo – but I was dead wrong. Bill drawled:

'Rich-aard,' he said it like my name had four syllables. 'List-en to me. After what I just learned about Leo if I was in the Now-rth Car-o-lina House there is no way I could vote for Leo Daughtry *under any circumstances.*'

A little while later I got a second call – from Joe Kiser.

He said Bill had called him too then laughed, 'Let me tell you what Leo and those boys have done now.'

After Leo and George and Ed had finished meeting with Black they'd made a beeline straight to the legislature and summoned Joe to George's office.

After Joe finished telling me about Leo's deal with Black, he said, 'That's what they want me to sell the caucus tomorrow.'

'You inclined to do it?'

'I believe I'm inclined to let them do it themselves.'

CHAPTER THIRTEEN
The Three A.M. Handshake

Black walked into the House Chamber the next morning dead-set on consummating the deal he'd made with Old Reliable, which in an outrage of fortune had slipped through his fingers the day before because Mary McAllister pressed the wrong button.

The clerk banged the gavel, calling the House to order and I stared across the rows of Republican legislators at an empty chair.

Old Reliable wasn't there.

He wasn't in the Chamber. He wasn't in the building. We were short one member. Which in a way was a relief. Because if Old Reliable wasn't there he couldn't vote for Black.

Joe Kiser stared at the same chair, stood up and made a motion to recess but Black had gotten over what must have been a moment of sheer outrage, staring at that same empty chair, long enough to figure out what he wanted too: For Old Reliable to walk through the door and sit in that chair and vote before that errant gene fired again.

In a way Jim Black and Cary Allred were like twins – but not identical twins. I think the first time Black laid eyes on Cary he saw a trait he'd never seen in another legislator. But he recognized it. He knew it like the back of his hand. Because he saw it staring back at him every day when he looked in the mirror. Because he'd been living with the same trait for years: Lust. Political lust. But not normal political lust a kind of high-octane rarified political lust that was pure rocket fuel and Jim had never seen it in anyone else so he just couldn't help being drawn to Cary.

But, in another way, he and Old Reliable they were like star-crossed lovers.

Because Jim's lust was constant, focused and relentlessly marching towards one fixed point: To be Speaker. While Old Reliable's lust had no fixed points – it was inflammable, mercurial, fickle and every time that errant gene fired, like a haywire gyroscope, he reeled off in a different direction leaving Black standing open-mouthed enraged.

The Democrats defeated Joe's motion to recess 60 to 59 then Joe led a filibuster to bring the House to a standstill and that suited Jim fine too. Because all he had to do was sit and listen to the filibuster and wait for Old Reliable to walk through the door – which he did about an hour later only by the look on his face he was a man in a complex state of mind. Old Reliable looked like he'd spent all night tossing and turning, weighing his lust for those twenty Committee Chairmanships he was going to appoint against a vague fear of the consequences – which he couldn't quite piece together – he was going to face after voting for Jim Black. So at dawn he was stuck between his lust egging him on and his fear hollering at him to stop.

He flopped into his chair. We held the sixth vote and as Black watched open-mouthed Old Reliable zigzagged again.

Then it was the Democrats who wanted a recess.

The House emptied and Black set off in hot pursuit of Old Reliable and Joe Kiser called a meeting of the Republican Caucus.

⌘

Joe walked to the center of the room and said Leo and George and Ed had hammered out an agreement with Jim Black and he'd let them explain it themselves.

Ed McMahan, standing by the wall at the side of the room drew himself up, puffed out his chest like a bantam rooster and pitched the deal like he was selling aluminum siding and said, *Here it is. We vote to make Black Speaker. Then the Democrats will vote for George for Speaker Pro Tempore* – the number two spot.

The explosion came concurrent with Ed's lips closing. The caucus erupted. Leo's own friends meant to lynch him. Every legislator in that room knew the man who was Speaker controlled the gavel and controlled the House.

When the howling stopped Leo's deal with Black was as dead as a doornail.

⌘

So at two o'clock when Black walked back onto the House floor one of his three deals was kaput and his on-again off-again deal with Old Reliable was off again.

He hardly blinked.

This time the Democrats moved that the House adjourn until Monday which gave Jim the whole weekend to pursue Old Reliable.

He still hadn't caught him by Monday so when the House met it recessed after four minutes – Tuesday was like deja-vu all over again. We met. And recessed again after four minutes.

By then even if Jim was a politician in lust he was also a sixty-eight year old man and all that stopping and starting, sitting and waiting, then dashing off in hot pursuit of Cary was beginning to wear him out and what weariness brought him was a glimmer of rational thought: When he saw himself being strapped to 'Old Reliable' for the next two years he began to think that might turn out to be his worst nightmare.

Plus he was facing a second problem.

The whole time he'd been pursuing Cary, Leo had been pursuing Martin Nesbitt and the block of dissidents in the Democratic caucus. Black had a nagging fear pursuing Old Reliable much longer might come at a pretty stiff price – Nesbitt might make his own deal with Leo, leaving Jim empty-handed.

⌘

That night around midnight I lifted the covers to climb into bed and the phone rang and Bill Culpepper said: 'We have to meet.'

'Now?'

I'd had a week of midnight phone calls and backroom deals and late-night skullduggery and it just didn't strike me right.

I didn't say it mean – in fact, I laughed as I said it – but I told Bill he should do something to himself that was anatomically impossible.

His voice dropped. 'Don't be that way.'

I snapped: 'You all should go on and make your deal with Leo. You'll get what you deserve.'

But Bill kept asking, saying we just had to meet that night, and sure enough temptation got the better of me.

I told him, Yes, hung up the phone, sat down on the bed and told myself, *Richard, you're the worst kind of fool.*

⌘

After Bill got there he wasn't in any hurry to get to what he had on his mind. Finally after an hour and a couple of stiff drinks he stretched his legs out in front of him and got down to brass tacks. He said Black wanted to hold one more roll call vote – to give him one last chance to win the Speakership outright – then after the vote he'd agree to share power. Bill said:

'I'll introduce the resolution myself.'

Then he took a sheet of paper – the resolution – out of his pocket and showed it to me and somewhere between two and three o'clock we shook hands on it.

CHAPTER FOURTEEN
The Eighth Day

The next morning the phone rang and it was Jim Black and I thought he was calling to confirm our agreement but instead he said, 'There's one problem. Five votes is not enough. Can you give me a bigger cushion?'

As far as Black knew I only had five votes, which was fine as long as his caucus stayed united. But now Black was afraid Martin Nesbitt and a handful of Democrats had made a deal with Leo. I said:

'Go on.'

'Can you get eight?'

'How about twelve?'

Black sounded surprised. 'I want to see their faces.'

⌘

At noon I sat down with twelve Republican legislators in the living room of my condominium and laid the cards on the table. When I finished I said, 'I guess the only thing left to say is if anyone's having second thoughts speak now or forever hold your peace.'

One of the legislators leaned forward on the sofa. 'This is a straight-up deal to share power?'

'You can ask Black yourself.'

Thirty minutes later Black and Culpepper walked through the door and Black started mumbling, saying we'd hold one more roll call vote and if the House was deadlocked we'd elect Co-Speakers and share power.

We headed back over to the legislature and the House convened and the clerk called the roll for the seventh ballot with everyone watching Old Reliable wondering if he was about to zigzag again.

He didn't.

The House deadlocked and Bill Culpepper stood up and said he had a resolution to share power and for one moment I felt like I was looking across Jordan at the Promised Land – then Ed McMahan sidled up to Old Reliable and whispered, 'Go on. If you'll vote for Black I will too' and in a heartbeat that errant gene fired and Old Reliable popped up and sang out, 'I move to reconsider that last vote' – which meant to hold the vote again.

Sitting, watching, I figured after a week of passing like two ships in the night Old Reliable's lust and Jim Black's lust had finally landed on the same spot at the same moment and all that was left was for the clerk to call the roll one last time.

⌘

Old Reliable sat down and got to thinking and faced a problem. The clerk called the roll in alphabetical order – so he was going to vote before McMahan. He was going to climb out on the limb first. Then he faced a second problem: What were the chances that Ed was going to climb out on that limb at all.

What would happen would be like domino's falling.

He would vote for Black.

Ed would double cross him and vote for George Holmes.

Black would be Speaker.

And there wouldn't be but one person to blame: Old Reliable.

Leo and Ed's hands would be clean.

It's hard to say what irritated him more. That fear that had stopped him every time he climbed up to the precipice of voting for Jim Black or the idea of Ed making a fool of him.

Either way that errant gene fired again.

They called the roll again Old Reliable voted for George and so did Ed McMahan.

It was the eighth deadlocked vote.

⌘

Culpepper didn't waste any time.

He stood up, stared across the House and said he was introducing a resolution for

Republicans and Democrats to share power, with Jim Black and Richard Morgan as Co-Speakers.

Half way through the roll call the dam broke. Sixty Democrats and twenty nine Republicans voted yes. The resolution passed 89 to 31.

Then Ed McMahan struck a final time.

One of Leo's allies stood up and roared out a motion to 'reconsider' – to rehold this vote too. Then Bill Culpepper stood up and said, 'I move to table that motion' – to kill another roll call.

In the back of the chamber Ed McMahan sprang to his feet, rushed down the aisle, crossed the House to Jim Black and – the way Black tells it – whispered, *Hold that vote again and we'll elect you Speaker alone.*

Art and Leo and Ed had talked a lot about loyalty to the caucus but less than a minute after the House elected a coalition where Republicans and Democrats would share power Ed McMahan tried to turn back the clock to make Jim Black Speaker alone.

Jim looked back at him and shook his head.

'You had your chance.'

CHAPTER FIFTEEN

Go Figure

There were no road maps or missals to guide us or tell us how Republicans and Democrats were to share power in the House but, in the end, we found our way by good old fashioned common sense.

Jim Black presided and wielded the gavel one day. I presided the next.

I appointed the Republican Committee Chairmen.

Jim appointed Democratic Co-Chairmen.

As far as practical politics went either Jim or I could block a bill. The Democrats wanted a lottery. I said no and the bill never came to a vote. They also wanted to pass a moratorium to end the death penalty – my no stopped it too.

But when I wanted to pass Tort Reform the shoe was on the other foot. Jim could say no and he did and stopped it.

One bill neither of us could stop was the budget which was awash in a sea of red ink: The state faced a billion-dollar deficit and the Co-speakership could have frozen into gridlock right there but it didn't and, in part, the reason was two very different women.

Dixie Epps and I had worked together day in and day out for years. Dixie was married to a highway patrolman, who later became an SBI agent, back in the 1990s when I persuaded her to leave her career job in the Department of Environment, Health and Natural Resources to become my Executive Assistant (ironically, one of her responsibilities in the Health Department involved the state's Pest Control Programs – which certainly qualified her to work in the legislature). She had a rare gift for cutting through knots and solving problems – in a male-dominated world – in a way that poured oil on troubled waters.

Sabra Faires had served as Legal Counsel to the House Finance Committee, then moved on to the Department of Revenue. Wiser men than I have floundered on the reefs and shoals of tax codes and revenue projections that shift like quicksand – after I persuaded her to come back to the General Assembly as my Chief of Staff she charted a course straight through the budget labyrinth and stuck to it, at times with feminine gentility and at other times with pure chutzpah.

When Sabra looked at the tax code to her it screamed for simplification – now 'tax streamlining' is an idea almost everyone is for until they read the details. Because the bottom line is while simplification means a lot of taxes go down it also, inevitably, means others go up.

Once sitting in my office facing Jim Black and Marc Basnight, arguing for her plan to 'streamline' the tax code, Sabra ran head-on into an unexpected problem. Jim Black loved candy and Dixie kept a drawer full of chocolate in my office and whenever Jim walked through the door he'd go straight to the drawer.

When I asked which taxes would go up under streamlining the first word out of Sabra's mouth – as Jim munched on a miniature Snickers bar – was candy.

The Democrats' solution to the deficit was to raise taxes.

I stopped that dead in its tracks.

But the Democrats stopped almost every bill to cut spending dead in it's tracks too.

In the end it boiled down to a fight over two taxes that were set to expire: A half-penny on the sales tax and a half-a-percent income tax on couples who earned over $200,000.

I wanted to end both but Black said, How do you do that and balance the budget? In the end we compromised and I got to eliminate the 'marriage penalty tax' and increase the child tax credit. Black got to keep the two taxes that were about to expire.

A year later, during my primary, Art Pope said my not letting those two taxes expire was the same as a tax increase.

I guess it's in the eye of the beholder.

No one's taxes went up. People paid the same taxes they had the year before. But they hadn't gotten a tax cut.

You decide who's right.

⌘

The other bill no one could stop was redistricting. Two years before, in 2001, when the Democrats had the majority the fight over redrawing legislators' districts had been bare-knuckled politics at it's worse. The Democrats had gerrymandered Republicans out of their seats by cutting counties into slivers and drawing lines snaking across maps.

The only way Republicans had to fight back was to file a lawsuit. They did and it dragged on a year and cost almost a million dollars but in the end a Democratic Judge –

Knox Jenkins – threw the Democrats plan out and redrew the districts himself.

So, in 2002, we ran in temporary districts and Republicans won sixty-one seats.

But in 2003 we had to start over – to redraw all the seats.

That fall we passed a plan N. C. Free, a bipartisan conservative business group, reported increased the number of 'Republican' districts from 49 to 55 – while the number of 'swing' districts and 'Democratic' districts dropped.

But the group that made maddest wasn't the Democrats: It was the lawyers lined up outside GOP Headquarters waiting to file another million-dollar lawsuit.

I'll tell you it's a flat-out fact: If you tell a Republican he's been fooled by a Democrat nine times out of ten he'll believe it. Those Republican 'redistricting' lawyers swung into action telling anyone who'd listen we'd passed a plan that didn't help Republicans – it hurt them. They said a plan creating six new

Republican districts was going to give Democrats control of the House and they got what they wanted. The party put up the money for another lawsuit.

By the end of the year the Republicans in the House had cut two taxes, balanced the budget with no tax increases, passed a redistricting plan that added Republican seats and in my primary Art Pope set out to defeat me by telling voters I'd betrayed Republican principles.

Go figure.

⌘

In the fall of 2004 Governor Easley rolled to victory over our candidate for governor and his coattails handed Jim Black a three vote majority in the House. In January of 2005 Jim Black returned to power as Speaker alone – then a subpoena from the United States Attorney rocked his world to its foundations.

CHAPTER SIXTEEN

The Poison Fruit

Sometimes you pull one thread and a whole garment unravels.

Jim Black passed the lottery in 2005, then the Raleigh *News and Observer* pulled a thread that led straight from a thirty-something brunette who worked for Black to a big Atlanta lottery company.

Meredith Norris started out in Jim's office in the legislature then she changed hats – Jim put her to work raising money for his campaigns and the Democratic Caucus.

But Meredith wasn't paid by Jim's campaign or the caucus. He had a better idea. He urged several corporations to hire Meredith and the one thing each of those corporations had in common was simple: Legislation.

When you boil away the camouflage Meredith was raising money for Jim, for instance from regional development organizations around the state, and they were paying her salary while she did it.

Jim got Meredith available – for free – whenever he needed her to handle a fundraiser and what the regional development organizations got – via Meredith – was a pipeline straight to Jim.

Meredith was, in effect, a lobbyist only according to her she didn't lobby. All she actually did she said – for instance for that Atlanta lottery company – was monitor legislation.

The *News and Observer* pulled that thread a little more and found out Meredith was a pretty extraordinary monitor. After the regional development organizations started paying her $66,000 a year bills passed the

House increasing the money they got from the state from $5.6 million to $8.5 million.

Next the *News and Observer* followed that thread through a Byzantine web of cogs and gears and levers to the heart of Black's fundraising machine and one of the people they found there was Alan Middleton, the Atlanta lottery company's Vice President.

The picture was clear: Meredith worked for Black and Middleton had hired her and gotten his own pipeline straight to Black's office.

From there the *News and Observer* followed the web straight from Middleton to Kevin Geddings – the man Black had appointed to the State Lottery Commission which was going to award the lottery contracts.

By law when Geddings was appointed he was required to file a financial report to disclose his conflicts of interest. According to his report he didn't have any.

When he talked to the *News and Observer* Geddings admitted he knew Middleton. They were acquaintances, friends, but they didn't do business together.

Then the second shoe fell: That wasn't exactly true – it turned out Geddings and Middleton had been long-time business associates in South Carolina.

Then the *News and Observer* marched over to the legislature and told Black's office they wanted to see his emails (which they had a right to do under the public information laws) and this time they found a smoking gun – Alan Middleton had written a section of the lottery legislation and Black's staff had put it in the bill. What that section did was simple: It made it harder for that Atlanta lottery company's biggest competitor to get lottery contracts.

A week later the United States Attorney rocked Black's world to the foundations with one word: Subpoena. A grand jury was investigating Black's appointment of Kevin

Geddings but that wasn't all: It was also investigating contributions to Black from video poker operators and Michael Decker's party switch.

FBI and SBI agents and grand juries begin looking in political nooks and crannies all over Raleigh and one of the facts they turned up was the Atlanta lottery company Kevin Geddings claimed he'd never had any business dealings with had actually paid him $229,000.

Jim Black had appointed a paid agent for a lottery company to the Lottery Board which handed out the state's contracts.

That was bad enough but Jim dug the hole deeper, telling reporters he barely knew Geddings which, naturally, led to the question, *Well, then, why did you appoint him?* Jim mumbled he couldn't remember quite where he got the idea.

That came out loud and clear at Geddings' trial: About the first words out of the U.S. Attorney's mouth were that Jim had picked Geddings over dinner at a Raleigh steakhouse with Alan Middleton – the lottery company vice president – and Meredith Norris.

A state court convicted Meredith, Geddings and Middleton of violating state lobbying laws. A federal court convicted Geddings of fraud and sentenced him to four years in prison and it looked like Jim Black was going to get his day in court next.

⌘

After Michael Decker switched parties, he lost his campaign for reelection. Months before the lottery scandal was even a cloud on the horizon the *News and Observer* reported how – after Decker's defeat – Black had gotten him a job that paid $48,000 in the Department of Cultural Resources.

When the U.S. Attorneys started digging into Black's fundraising, looking for ties between Black and Meredith and the Atlanta lottery company they ran head-on into a stack of contributions Black had given Decker when he changed parties.

Then the State Board of Elections cranked up its own investigation and ran into that same stack of contributions and found an odd thing – those checks had two different sets of handwriting on them.

For years – it turned out – Jim and the Optometrist Political Action Committee (Jim was an optometrist himself) had been working hand-in-glove in a pretty peculiar way – the PAC would collect checks from optometrists all over the state with the amounts written in but the payee line left blank. Then Jim and the PAC's treasurer would decide which candidates to give them to and fill in the blank line.

When Jim testified at the hearing he looked the Chairman of the State Board of Elections straight in the eye and said he'd never filled in a single one of those contributions.

The Chairman handed him a check.

'Look at the payee line. Do you recognize the handwriting?'

Jim was caught red-handed. He'd written the check – to Michael Decker's campaign right after he switched parties.

By the time the Board called Decker his lawyer had already told him about the last thing on earth he ought to do was to say one word about those checks so standing there with the whole state of North Carolina watching the man who'd switched parties to make Jim Black Speaker took the Fifth Amendment.

When the Board finished with the optometrists they moved on to video poker operators – who had given Jim $120,000 in campaign contributions. One of the first witnesses, a young woman who worked as a clerk in a convenience store in Laurinburg, told the Board she'd been given $2,500 in cash by the video poker operator who owned the store and told her to send the money to Jim Black in her name.

⌘

Michael Decker stiffing the Board of Elections by taking the Fifth was one thing but dodging a United States Attorney with a battalion of FBI agents was another.

One morning Decker walked into federal court and told the strangest story of all: How in the weeks after Leo had double-crossed him at the Republican Caucus he'd driven to an IHOP in Salisbury, twice, to meet with Jim Black and then he said he'd agreed to switch parties in exchange for $50,000 – $38,000 in checks and $12,000 in cash – dressed up as campaign contributions, plus a $44,000-a-year job for his son.

Black's answer to that was blunt. He said – or his lawyer said – there are liars and damn liars and Decker had lied so he could cut a better deal from the prosecutors.

The judge sentenced Decker to prison for four years.

⌘

No one saw the last scandal coming.

In 2005 Jim had inserted a line in the 400-page state budget that said insurance companies had to treat chiropractors the same way they did family doctors. What that meant was if a patient's co-payment to see his family doctor was twenty dollars he'd pay the same amount to see a chiropractor – which made it a lot cheaper to visit a chiropractor, which the way chiropractors saw it put money in their pockets.

Two years later when just about everyone was waiting for Jim to get indicted for bribing Mike Decker or putting Kevin Geddings on the Lottery Board, instead he walked into a federal courtroom and stunned everyone by admitting he'd taken $29,000 from chiropractors and put it in his pocket for putting that line in the state budget.

The judge sentenced Jim Black to five years in prison.

⌘

It's hard to describe how I feel about what Jim did today. I served beside him two years as Speaker. I worked with him every day. He was my friend. How I don't feel is outraged. Or holier than thou. A day comes when unless you're blind you can't avoid seeing what every saint who ever drew breath figured out: Sin is bone deep. It's wider than any ocean. And none of us is safe. A thirty-year-old girl was foolish enough to believe monitoring legislation wasn't lobbying. A history teacher from the Gospel Light Christian School, in an IHOP in Salisbury, took a $50,000 bribe. And a 72-year-old grandfather is serving five years in prison.

I guess how I feel about it is like the sinner's prayer, 'Have mercy, oh Lord, on me a sinner.'

CHAPTER SEVENTEEN
An Alien World

When it rains it pours.

On Election Day in November of 2006 after I voted I came home and opened my mailbox and inside was a note from an FBI agent. I walked into the house and called him and he said he had a subpoena for me to testify in front of the Grand Jury.

I looked down at the phone. 'Well, I don't see any point in you driving all the way back down here. Would you like me to pick it up tomorrow when I'm in Raleigh?'

The next day I rolled to a stop in front of the federal building, got out of my car and he walked out of the building and handed me the subpoena.

Now, if you think what goes on in front of a Grand Jury is secret you're only partly right – it wasn't an hour before the first reporter called and I'll tell you a fact that's as true as sin being bone deep: There's no reason on earth you can give a reporter for being subpoenaed to testify before a Grand Jury that doesn't sound like you're guilty of something.

That subpoena was a long list of names and the U.S. Attorney wanted to know everything I knew about any of them. Well, I knew Jim Black and Michael Decker and I thought I recognized the name of a video poker operator Leo had once represented but I didn't know hardly any of the other names.

I also knew George Holding, the U.S. Attorney – not well, but well enough to be sure of two things: If George's best friend were called to testify in front of the Grand Jury George wouldn't cut him any slack and if I was innocent he would figure it out. So I just figured I'd drive up to the Grand Jury and let George ask his questions.

It turned out I was the only one who thought that made any kind of sense at all. My lawyer looked me straight in the face and asked if I would like a list of innocent men indicted by Grand Juries.

That got my attention enough to hire a criminal attorney, then I set about answering the subpoena.

In addition to the names George had asked for financial records going back years – checks, bank statements, tax returns, emails, letters.

I had the folks in the legislature dump all the emails I'd sent or received onto a disk and shipped it over to the U.S. Attorney's office. I started to sort through years of financial records then decided, instead of making copies, the simplest solution was to stack them in boxes and just send the originals to Raleigh.

Today, describing it, that doesn't sound like much but you have to go through it to know how it feels. I had complete strangers pouring over every penny I'd spent for years. Looking at what my wife spent on groceries. What I paid my doctor. Every tax deduction. Every penny anyone had paid me. Every penny I owed. Just saying that is an invasion of privacy has a hollow ring. It doesn't cover the sense of violation you feel.

The day of the hearing my attorney and I crossed the street to the federal building; a lady who worked for the U.S. Attorney met us in the lobby and led us into an elevator then down a hallway and left us in a waiting room. I sat staring at the walls until John Bruce, the Senior Assistant U.S. Attorney, came in and he looked more like a college professor or teacher than a bare-knuckled prosecutor. He led me into a small hall – like an auditorium – and I sat down and faced the Grand Jury.

This isn't well known but about the only place in America you can't take your lawyer is into a Grand Jury hearing. You're in there all alone facing a battery of prosecutors and the jurors.

I was sitting on a kind of stage with a roll-down movie screen behind me and the stenographer and the attorneys in front of me and John stood up, glanced down at a pad.

'Mr. Morgan, do you remember when you learned Michael Decker had switched parties?'

That had been four years ago. 'The same time everyone else did. From the newspapers.'

An attorney turned on a projector and put a newspaper article up on the screen from *The Winston Salem Journal* about Decker's party switch and asked if I had seen it.

'Either that one or one like it.'

Halfway through that hearing something struck me as odd – those lawyers who'd convicted drug pushers and embezzlers and pornographers, who'd seen every kind of sin were genuinely puzzled by the workings of politics – those U.S. Attorneys were staring into an alien world and trying to figure out how it worked and to them it was making no sense at all.

John Bruce asked about the Co-Speakership. How did it come about? How did it work day to day? Who made the decisions? I know this is naive but I couldn't help but thinking most of those questions were just plain curiosity – that I was sitting there because he'd encountered a mystery and meant to puzzle it out.

My attorney had told me what lawyers always say: When you testify give short concise answers. A lawyer's idea of an answer is blunt and simple: You say yes or no and shut up. I didn't even try.

After an hour John Bruce stopped, looked down at his pad, and said he was done and I thought, *That's it? That's all?* Next one or two of the Grand Jurors asked questions – and it struck me they were just as puzzled and intrigued by that alien world as those lawyers.

Then they excused me and I left the room and I haven't heard a word from them since.

The real problem I faced head-on that year wasn't Grand Juries – it was politics.

CHAPTER EIGHTEEN
Lies Have Wings

Two years before I testified before the Grand Jury, back when I was still Speaker, Art had fired the first salvo in his jihad to defeat me in my 2004 primary.

At the Republican State Convention he – and his allies –returned to one of his favorite topics: That Republican legislators owed a sacred allegiance to vote with the caucus.

But when his allies introduced a resolution requiring loyalty oaths they went too far for party leaders like former Governor Martin and Senator Elizabeth Dole.

You have to stop a minute to think to realize what a bad idea it is to require a loyalty oath to a political party.

The United States Senate, the Congress, no political party in the United States I am aware of has ever required a loyalty oath.

What a loyalty oath comes down to is simple: One man sets the party line – and tells another man what to do.

How many people do you know who you would swear an oath to follow blindly?

Would you swear an oath to follow the Republican Party blindly? Or any party?

Well with Art pouring gas on the fire, that's exactly what delegates voted to require Republican legislators to do: Swear a blind oath of loyalty to the Republican party.

Politics is not always an exercise in truth and in my primary in 2004 Art defined my 'disloyalty' to the Republican Party this way: He said when Republicans had a majority in the House I voted to elect a Democrat Speaker, not a Republican. I was what he called a R.I.N.O. – a Republican in Name Only and he was the voice of the Republican Party.

He left out that after Decker's switch we no longer had a majority. And that Leo had tried to make a deal with Black.

Since 1996 I'd counted on Mark Stephens and Paul Shumaker to run my campaigns. But, in 2004, Mark was leading Senator Elizabeth Dole's political organization and Senator Dole could only lose by getting in the middle of an inner-party fight with people who had supported her on both sides. Paul Shumaker tried to help but he was working for Richard Burr's 2004 campaign for Senate and, in the end, he was spread pretty thin. So when it came to building a campaign team I almost had to start over from scratch. But that wasn't my biggest problem. The biggest problem was more basic: Money. I had to raise it while all Art had to do was write a check.

During the primary he poured hundreds of thousands of dollars into his campaign to defeat me and campaigns to defeat other Republican legislators he said were disloyal.

I won but three other Republican legislators lost their primaries and a chill settled over the House: Art had sent a blunt message to the remaining Republican legislators: Being my friend meant being his enemy. And he'd just proved he'd spend half a million dollars to defeat my friends in their primaries.

Art hadn't beat me but he had accomplished a more subtle goal: He'd driven a wedge between me and other legislators and taken the first step toward leaving me isolated in the House.

⌘

In 2004 during my primary Art could say I had served as Co-Speaker with a Democrat. In 2006 he could say something worse: I had served as Co-Speaker with a crook.

The scandals engulfing Jim Black didn't start until months after I left office as Speaker but the hard fact, politically, was standing on a dais for two years by Jim Black had put a brand on me: The scandals had turned him into the biggest skunk in North Carolina politics and the smell was just bound to stick to me.

And Art was putting together just the kind of campaign to be sure. Back in 1996 – just after they'd left The Club to start their own company – I'd hired Bob Rosser and Calvin Kervin to work in the House campaigns along with Mark Stephens. I worked with Bob and Calvin in every election for the next five years.

But in 2006 they were working for Art and so was Mark's partner, Tom Fetzer – Art had more of my political team working for him than I did and I don't know which was the greater shock, to find my old friends leading a campaign to defeat me or what they said in their ads.

The mailings started two months before the election and didn't stop. One had a picture of a man standing in a shadow with his face hidden – so anyone who didn't know better would think it was me – holding a burlap sack, like those bags you see stacked in Brink's trucks, and the message was brutal: Jim Black was a crook and so was I.

Another had a picture of a hand – my hand – turning the dial of a safe full of money. Two other ads had pictures of me in front of mounds of cash.

Another had a man who looked like a prisoner in a dark room looking up at a skylight – the caption said Richard Morgan has a lot to hide. There were ads with pictures of me and Jim Black and the words 'Sold Out' stamped above my picture and ads with playing cards with my picture and Blacks picture on the cards beside the words 'Two of a Kind.' Another had a dime on the front and said there wasn't a dime's worth of difference between me and Jim Black.

Art unleashed a tidal wave of money and ads and what they all said was Richard Morgan voted to elect Democrat Jim Black Speaker, Richard Morgan turned his back on

Republicans, Richard Morgan handed power to the Democrats.

In 2003 when I was battling Leo for the Speakership, Bill Cobey – the Republican Party Chairman – had called me and said if he were sitting in the State House there was no way he would vote for Leo Daughtry 'under any circumstances.'

During my primary Bill came to Southern Pines with a couple of former state chairmen to campaign for my opponent.

At that rally I was compared to Adolf Hitler.

A grave robber.

A child molester.

"The only difference," former Chairman Frank Rouse told the crowd, "Between Richard Morgan and Al Capone was Al Capone died of syphilis."

And they said a prayer asking God to see to it I lost.

I said earlier in most campaigns it's not what your opponent does that beats you, it's what you do to beat yourself. I beat myself.

Ostriches aren't the only animals who stick their heads into the sand. I learned a hard fact of human nature. When you hear all that venom about yourself its natural to recoil and tell yourself no one will believe it. And that's a mistake.

In politics lies have wings.

When a loud-mouthed bully calls you a child molester you'd better leave no doubt in anyone's mind how you feel about it.

My mistake was simple and lethal: I ignored those attacks.

⌘

On election night we gathered at my office – there were people filling the room who'd been there every election night for sixteen years – in Pinehurst. My wife was talking with a circle of women, volunteers, when the phone rang and she picked it up and a reporter asked what she thought of me losing. She said it wasn't true. The returns weren't all in. Then she walked into the other room where I was looking at the returns on a computer and I told her, Yes, it's true.

I think from then on it was like the story of *The Gift of the Magi*. I was worried about how she would take it – while she was worried about me.

That night for the first time she'd run for office. She won. I felt my loss blighted that for her. And, on her side, she would have traded her victory for my defeat.

The odd thing that night was I felt no anger. What weighed on me – like regret – were the webs of lies and venom and poison and spite.

Then right there amid all the squalor I discovered a nugget of pure gold. This is the price you pay for climbing into the arena: Defeat. But what I was asking myself standing there on election night tarred and feathered, beaten, in the last ditch, wasn't how I was going to live with it but how my wife would endure it. Nothing else mattered. The rest was just noise and politics. Cindy laid her hand on my chest and leaned against my shoulder and I knew, right then, everything was going to be just fine.

All that was left was for me to speak to the volunteers staring numbly at televisions to give them some kind of closure because, finally, in defeat the last trap you have to avoid is bitterness.

I faced my friends and neighbors and a row of cameras and reporters and told them it was a hard blow but blessings come from defeats.

CHAPTER NINETEEN
Art's Jihad

Leo, at sixty-seven, moving a little slower, sedate, still sits in the House, quietly holding his seat with the vices and virtues of an aging politician.

Art, more than Leo, carried on the jihad after 2003 until he finally defeated me.

A week or so before the election I learned Art wasn't paying for most of his ads out of his own pocket, he was paying for them out of two of The Pope Family corporations – which under North Carolina law is illegal. But Art had found a loophole.

The courts say if a corporation has something to say about an issue – like raising taxes – that's fine. It's perfectly legal. It's their

God-given right under the First Amendment of the Constitution. But what is illegal is for a corporation to spend money to defeat a candidate.

The point in that law is subtle but has a certain reasonableness behind it: A corporation – say an oil company – has a right to say anything it wants about energy policy but since it's not a good idea to have corporations electing people who'll vote to give them subsidies they can't spend one dollar on an election.

Which sounds fine. But leads to a knotty problem: Because figuring out the difference – between 'fine' and 'illegal' – in the turmoil of a political campaign is like counting the number of angels that can dance on the head of a pin. The answer is intriguing but elusive.

Art never made any bones about what he set out to do: He wanted me out of office. So I wrote the Elections Board and said it looked pretty clear to me he'd been running those ads to defeat me.

After the primary the Board held a hearing and Art climbed onto the witness stand and took the oath and said I was dead wrong. He said he'd read the law and knew the law and swore he'd never run a single one of his ads to defeat me – so the ads were perfectly legal.

But, in the end, I suspect Art may find – as I did when Jerry Whipple ran off with the dispatcher in the sheriff's office – victory can be more treacherous than defeat.

Looking back I think when Art and I parted company wasn't the day I ran for Speaker – it was years before when he tramped into my office and rapped that list down on my desk and snapped that's what The Pope Family had given to elect Republicans.

In an odd way I think Art valued that list like those old French nobles in the Ancient Regime valued their titles. In a French grandee's eyes back then titles in and of themselves had virtue – they didn't reflect virtue but inherently had it and the moment a fellow was anointed Count or Duke that virtue became as much a part of him as the air he breathed. It set him apart. That list was part of the air Art breathed. It set him apart. It had virtue. And the act of giving was a virtue but the minute he thumped that list down on my desk even a blind man could see his reason for giving was no virtue at all. So when I looked back at him and told him no it was like saying the Emperor had no clothes.

And, of course, his natural reaction was to pick up the nearest political axe and start flailing away and that was when he discovered a sure fire way to get respect: Fear.

How that worked was a story old as the hills: I lost and other legislators got the message loud and clear – cross Art at your own risk. He beat me. He could beat you.

After that fear spawned tangible fruit: Every time Art growled it sent a tremor through Republican legislators.

But, over time, I suspect Art will find he's built on a shaky foundation – because, in the end, fear breeds enemies. It breeds more enemies every day.

CHAPTER TWENTY

The Fourth Witch

Taking a forced sabbatical from politics has been a blessing in almost every way. My life returned to a pace and rhythm I had forgotten existed. No more midnight meetings. No more back room deals, no pressure so thick you could cut it with a knife. No more climbing into bed exhausted and waking up the morning still tired.

Before the election I was diabetic which, if I'd stopped long enough to listen, I should have seen as a warning sign only a fool would ignore. Cindy had been telling me for years, 'Richard it's like little termites eating at you. When are you going to do something about it?' After the election at last I sat still long enough to read the papers she'd been giving me about diabetes and got the message loud and clear.

A year later, after more lifestyle changes than any fifty-six-year-old man ought to be required to put up with diabetes and I have parted company – at least for now.

It was about that time I picked up the phone and called Carter and said, *Don't you think it's time we buried the hatchet?*

Since that night about once each week I drive up to Raleigh and the two of us have dinner and mostly we spend hours picking over the bones of thirty years of politics and sinning.

As young men – in our innocence – we know our hearts are pure and our cause's sacred then, years later, we look back and see purity was a phantom and we pursued our causes amid wastelands of squalor.

St. Paul on the road to Damascus was struck speechless by a flash of light then in one crystal moment heard Christ's voice. My wife's father – a Baptist preacher – would call that revealed truth.

I have friends who know the moment and place and time of day when they saw the light and what they were thinking and feeling and praying the second before.

But I think epiphany doesn't come to many men in a flash of light – it comes instead by inches, over years, measured in grief and sin until at last so worn out the game hardly seems worth the candle we stop and ask ourselves, *Will it ever end?*

In the next breath we begin a pilgrimage and find out the answer is, no, it never ends. None of our hands are clean.

Not Leo's or Art's or mine – because when it came to Jim Black, Art was right but not in the way he said.

My sin wasn't that I agreed to share power with Jim. It was in my not looking him in the eye, later, and saying, *I can read a newspaper report. Is it true you bribed Mike Decker?*

Instead I didn't ask. Because Jim was my friend I closed my eyes – and I'll warn you the easiest sin you'll ever commit is the one where you don't have to say a word or lift a finger – where all you have to do is close your eyes.

There's a story from *The Acts of King Arthur and His Noble Knights* where Sir Lancelot is captured by four witches who tell him he must choose one of them to marry.

Then each witch shows him a vision of why he should pick her over her sisters.

The first witch – and these witches were beautiful women – transforms herself into the Dark Ages vision of Marilyn Monroe or Helen of Troy and what she promises Lancelot is what every man dreams of.

The second witch conjures a vision of mountains of gold and jewels and rubies and sapphires and offers Lancelot the wealth of Midas.

The third witch offers him a vision of eternal fame – Lancelot's name will live for a thousand years.

The fourth witch – the witch Queen Morgan le Fay – offers Lancelot no vision at all. Instead she whispers in his ear, 'I will give you power because with power you can have these other three.'

Sir Lancelot high-tailed it right out of there. He figured that last temptation was too much for anyone to resist.

The temptation that frightened Lancelot and corrupted Jim Black is alive and well. It lives and breathes. Every day. In politics.

The day you finally ask yourself, *Are my hands clean*, there is a reckoning and that's a sad and happy day because you wake up the next morning in a fallen world full of grays where nothing that walks on two legs can lay claim to a pure heart and truth is not found in blacks and whites but in the shadows, staring back at us alongside our sins – then in the next breath you see lying in the weeds amid the squalor a kind of miracle.

On one corner of an intersection on a country road not far from my home are two tiny crosses – where two teenage girls died. One of those girls' mothers grieved herself to death a year later.

One night when I came home from Raleigh, after I finished telling my wife all about billion dollar budget deficits or lottery scandals or whatever mountains we'd beaten into mole hills that week in the legislature she folded her arms across her chest and said practically, *Well, that's all fine and good but when are you going to do something about that intersection?*

When I drive beneath the flashing warning light at that intersection, every time I look at those crosses it is an affirmation amid all that sinning blessings flowed and rolled on like a river of grace.

CHAPTER TWENTY-ONE
Epilogue

A year and a half after I lost my primary friends started talking to me about running for State House again. I thought about it and while I was thinking one morning the telephone rang.

Joe Boylan – the man who'd beaten me in 2006 – had just been arrested by a state trooper for drunk driving, which made temptation a little stronger.

In the end the answer was simple: I'd been walking one road for sixteen years. I wanted to walk in a different direction.

Instead, after a lot of thought, I filed for State Superintendent of Public Instruction, a race where the stars have to align for me to win.

Why Superintendent of Public Instruction?

Well, the schools are a challenge worth going to work on.

The primary was a pleasant surprise. I spent hardly any money and carried 97 counties.

Maybe lightning will strike again – we'll see. It depends on whether people are really set on change.

A friend, a Democrat, gave me a pretty good idea. He told me a story about Charlie Crist, the Governor of Florida. A reporter cornered Crist and demanded to know how he was going to straighten out the schools and Crist stared back at him and said that was easy, the best thing he could do for the schools was to have people lined up at the doors to be teachers but to do it they'd have to pay teachers more. A lot more.

The reporter snapped how on earth did Crist figure he was going to pay for that and Crist said do the math, they'd take the money spent on bureaucracy, cut it, and have all the money they needed.

I've looked at the North Carolina education budget and I'll tell you, a Ph.D. from Harvard couldn't figure out how much we spend on bureaucracy. The money's hidden so well it could take years to find.

But Charlie Crist is right. Better teachers do mean better schools and somewhere there's an Einstein-like genius who can figure out how much we spend on bureaucracy and how much we can cut so we can pay teachers more.

And I'll tell you one other problem I'd like to figure out. I reckon this isn't politically correct to say and I expect it is not popular either but another big problem in our schools is a kind of politics called social engineering.

Last year North Carolina eight-graders took the national writing exam and we were the *only* state in the nation where test scores dropped. The bottom line was pretty blunt: 71% of our students are not proficient in writing and 30% to 40% – no one knows the exact number – drop out of school, while we spend $10 billion on public education each year.

That seems more important to me than turning our schools into social laboratories.

Let's get the schools out of the social engineering business and back to being sure eighth graders can write.

We can do that by getting just a little of the sinning out of politics.

Acknowledgments

One night at dinner a friend asked my wife, Cindy, which fields of nursing she'd worked in. She said she'd been an E.R. nurse, a surgical nurse, a nurse administrator, a home care nurse, a hospice volunteer and, oh yes, she'd worked in the psychiatric ward at our local hospital...my friend stopped her right there and laughed.

'That last one certainly prepared you for your marriage.'

About the best thing any fellow can do is over-marry himself. I certainly did. And it is a blessing I count every day.

From genesis to completion of this book Cindy did everything from reading the manuscripts to digging through old files late at night looking for long-buried documents.

I also owe a special thanks to Representative Joe Kiser, who served as House Republican Leader while I was Speaker. Remembering the intricacies of Republican caucuses is confusing and Joe's memory added needed clarity. What I have reported accurately is due to Joe. Any mistakes are my own.

And I'd also like to express my gratitude to former Representative Bill Culpepper. Bill, who is a respected Democrat, served as Rules Committee Chairman under Jim Black and I during the years Jim and I were Co-Speakers. I am grateful to him for filling in gaps in my memory about the race for Speaker in 2003 and, especially, for sharing the Democrats' perspective on the race. Again, what I have reported accurately is due to Bill. The mistakes are my own.

Special thanks are also due to Donna Haywood; Donna worked with me in my business during the 1980s and 1990s and when I was away in Raleigh more or less ran the business single-handedly. She has also, over the last decade, filed a mountain of campaign reports with the State Board of Elections each time I have run for office. I would also like to express my gratitude to Dixie Epps, who lived through most of the events in the book while working with me in the General Assembly, and to Sabra Faires, who was my Chief of Staff during the years I was Speaker.

And for their time, suggestions and diligence, my heartfelt thanks to Acree Graham and Emily Wrenn.

One word needs to be said about the dialog in the book. I don't pretend to be able to remember verbatim conversations from twenty years ago. I have put quotes in single parentheses because I have paraphrased as accurately as memory allows.

Lastly, this book would not exist without Carter Wrenn. One night last summer, while we were talking about my campaign for Superintendent of Public Instruction, he said, 'Look, one of the most important things you could do this fall is write your book. You can tell people a story no one else can and that story will help them understand politics – beyond the next election. That's as important as ads, speeches, or debates.'

Then he turned around and asked me to do a campaign debate – but that's another story.

Anyway, I thought over his suggestion and it made sense to me.

Since then Carter and I have spent many late nights chewing over our shared thirty years in politics and his hand is on every page in this book. I knew the story. He knew how to tell it. I would also like to thank his long-suffering wife, Page, for sharing him all those evenings.

When you walk in Carter's office, after you cross a small lobby, you walk through a pair of double doors into a large library. It was there Carter introduced me to John Steinbeck's *The Acts of King Arthur and His Noble Knights* and the fourth witch. She said it all.

www.ingramcontent.com/pod-product-compliance
Lightning Source LLC
Chambersburg PA
CBHW021229090426
42740CB00006B/447